A Daydreamer's Digest

Tales from the Berkshires

Whimsical Stories by Richard C Henneberry

Copyright © 2012 Richard C Henneberry

All rights reserved.

ISBN: 978-0615700137

Published in the United States by
DayDreamer Press
Viera, Florida

To Pat

With Thanks for our fifty-three years together

And Hopes for fifty-three more.

Illustrations by
Patricia Henneberry
Patrick Henneberry
Eliza Henneberry

Photographs by the Author
Cover Photo: Sleepy Hollow Road, Richmond, MA

Contents

PREFACE

When I was young, an aspiring writer growing up in the Berkshires had many stellar examples to follow. When it came to fiction, the ghosts of Melville, Hawthorne, Wharton and many more were all around us. Local treasures such as Hal Borland, Morgan Bulkeley Sr., and Milton Bass showed us the way to address more down-to-earth issues. Bass's broad range of writings - from his experiences in WWII to the health of his garden to national politics - encouraged me to think that my experiences and opinions might actually be of some interest to others.

With these models available to me, who influenced me the most? Not so much the novelists; they were important to me, but Mark Twain, James Thurber and Harry Golden were my main guys. Twain's short stories stuck in my head, Thurber's chaotic pieces made me laugh as often as I returned to them, and Golden's essays helped steer my conscience through some tumultuous times in our Nation's history. Recently, Kevin O'Hara's career has taken off, proving that a Pittsfield kid who came up through the local parochial schools can become a successful and widely-acclaimed author. O'Hara's success, arriving rather late in life, resonates with an old-timer like me from the same city, with the same school background and an equally full set of Irish genes.

As I became established in my scientific career, I was able to set aside a little time to write for pleasure. The short pieces in this book, which can only be described as an eclectic collection, were written since then. Some of them go back 20 years (Liam will be 21 next spring). The stories are all based on actual events - whatever popped up and caught my fancy. The topics largely reflect my interests in family life and my involvements in flying, skiing and restoring old sports cars. And yes, in a few of the stories a little science sneaks in. Occasionally, my curmudgeon's side reveals itself, but most of the pieces deal with trivial subjects and I have attempted to present them in a whimsical manner.

Now, as I solidify my credentials as a senior citizen, with the encouragement of my wife and the advent of innovative ways to publish electronically, I have decided to pull a few of my favorite old stories together in the hope that someone will read them. Some of them still make me laugh. I hope they will have the same effect on you.

Canaan, New York, August 10, 2012

A Daydreamer's Digest

Tales from the Berkshires

Published by

DayDreamer Press

Viera Florida

1

Ellen's Package

1

Ellen's Package

When a house is listed for sale with a real estate agent in this area, the agent often hosts an Open House for other agents in the vicinity. Realtors figure that the more people showing the house to prospective buyers, the more likely it is to sell and then everybody is happy. To attract as many real estate people as possible to the open house, some agencies lay on a free lunch.

When we listed our home for sale with our friend Mel, he pulled out all the stops on a fancy lunch hoping to attract dozens of hungry agents. On the big day, Mel arrived about thirty minutes early to set up all the goodies. Lately, he never travels alone. Not since his new puppy, Cowboy, rode into town. At nine months old, Cowboy tips the scales at 80 pounds already and promises to top out about 120. As well-known dog lovers of all sizes and all kinds we always welcome Cowboy to our spread to cavort with our rambunctious canine, Skete. So while Mel went about his lunch preparations and Pat finished up some last-minute cleanup chores, Cowboy and Skete went about their favorite game - which seems to involve taking turns at biting each other's neck while they roll in the muddiest spot they can find. They had the entire six acres to play in, at least until the rain started - which it did just as the first agents arrived. I called the dogs inside. At the same time, just when Pat thought she had the clutter under control, the UPS truck showed up with a large package from our daughter Ellen.

As my contribution to sprucing up the place for the agents, I decided to open Ellen's package and get rid of the unsightly packing material. But the moment I began to open the box, I detected a strong, strange, and decidedly unpleasant odor. I folded back both flaps of the box and the odor increased alarmingly. Just as I bent over to gently sniff the contents, two of Mel's guest agents came down the stairs munching away on the free lunch. At least they were munching away until suddenly one of them began to gag and bolted for the door. The other one looked at me rather strangely for a moment as tears began to roll down his cheeks, then he tore off after his friend, lunch forgotten.

By this point I was beginning to feel a wave of nausea rolling over me, but I went back to Ellen's package and gingerly lifted some of the packing materials out of the way. It seemed that every time I touched the box, the horrible odor intensified. Had Ellen sent us some tasty surprise that had spoiled en route? Could rotten fudge smell that bad? What else could smell so bad and still fit in the box? Was it a practical joke? Or had Ellen's cat snuck into the box and been trapped, only to expire in the back of a UPS truck crossing Oklahoma and become a putrefied stink bomb before finally reaching us in the Berkshires?

I had begun to stuff the packaging back in the box just as an agent I recognized came sauntering into the room. She had the profile of a person who seldom missed a free lunch, and with a mouth fairly full of roast beef she offered what was probably meant to sound like a cheerful greeting. At least it started out sounding like a cheerful greeting, until she began to assume a dangerous shade of green and showed early symptoms of terminal gagging. I tried to return her greeting but I decided I had only a few moments left before I would unceremoniously lose the lunch I hadn't even eaten yet. It was better not to try to talk.

I figured my best bet was to get Ellen's package out of the house before noxious liquids started dripping from the bottom of the box, saturating the rugs and furniture with an odor that could never be eliminated. I had visions of the word spreading like wildfire among real estate agents: "Don't bring anybody near that house, you'd never believe the smell inside!". We would have to take the house off the market, buy gallons of AirWick, and leave the windows wide open all winter long! Could we wash the whole house with tomato juice, as if a skunk had gone on a spraying spree in the family room?

I raced for the door with Ellen's package held at arms length before me, my only thought being to get the malodorous object out of the house before the contamination was a permanent feature of our suddenly unmarketable home. Unfortunately, the box and I reached the door just as two arriving real estate agents started into the house. We collided and crashed in a pungent pile to the floor in a flurry of packing materials and real estate forms. Bent on survival at any cost, I scurried on all fours out into the blessedly fresh air and, still on hands and knees, breathed deeply for several minutes - oblivious to the gentle rain. Ellen's package lay twenty feet away, harmless enough unless the wind shifted. The two agents I had sent scrambling, meanwhile, came stumbling over me hands over mouths as they scrambled for the safety of the clear Berkshire air. Just as I tried again to get up, who should go leaping over me but our dog Skete; she seemed as eager to vacate the premises as the real estate agents had been. Skete's behavior should have alerted me, but there was no time to think.

All hell broke loose as most of the real estate agents bolted for their cars while emitting strange retching and gurgling sounds. Skete stood blocking the driveway and barking her loudest, deepest, and most authoritative barks, while Cowboy stood watching her with a perplexed look. Frantic agents spun their wheels in the wet grass as they sought shortcuts over what passes for our front lawn but is really a pasture and not at all hospitable to automobiles. Several cars became stuck in the holes I never got around to filling. Serious cursing could be heard, mixed with great gasps for breath as the lunch guests, most of whom were by then an unbecoming shade of purple, took their leave any way they could.

I expected to see an unscheduled visit from the Health Department at any moment but it was the volunteer fire department that actually arrived with sirens, flashing lights, bullhorn and all. It seems a late-arriving agent panicked and used his car phone to call 911 on seeing the commotion spilling from our doorways.

Then, as suddenly as it had begun, the mystery of Ellen's package was solved. At the peak of the pandemonium Pat's voice - which I could tell was only a decibel or two from total panic - was heard to exclaim over the melee: "Cowboy, you bad dog! Go outside!"

As the few remaining real estate agents watched in amazement, each frozen in place with one hand holding a sandwich while the other hand covered his or her mouth, I raced into the house to see what had grabbed Pat's attention. The odor nearly overwhelmed me as I finally stood face-to-face with the granddaddy of all stink bombs; Cowboy, the 80 pound puppy, had innocently answered nature's call on the family room rug. Wavy green lines just like those in the comic strips emanated upward and outward from the most enormous pile I had ever seen a puppy deposit, a pile any circus elephant would be proud of. The stench was a phenomenon no human should be asked to bear. The doorway was suddenly jammed with bodies struggling to get out of the soon-to-be condemned house.

Within a few weeks the air cleared at our house and Ellen's package was off the hook. Cowboy, who promised to be more careful, was again welcome to keep Skete company although we encourage them to spend more time outdoors, preferably downwind from the house. But strangely enough, none of those real estate agents who stopped by for a free lunch has ever been back to show our gracious home to prospective buyers. And I threw away the wrappings from Ellen's unfairly-accused package; the very sight of them was enough to start me gagging all over again.

The End

Cryin' on the Outside

2

Cryin' on the Outside

The day started out sunny with temperatures in the mid-40s, surprisingly warm for mid-March in the Berkshires. The next surprise was that it stayed that way all day, and it's a lucky thing for me that it did.

Our dog began her usual frenetic barking when the FedEx truck rolled into the yard. Her carrying-on is something you don't really get use to, but I figure society must be responsible for her being this neurotic so what can I do? As I often do when a delivery arrives, I stepped out onto the second-story deck, closed the sliding door behind me to contain the wild beast, and stretched down to get the parcel the FedEx agent handed up to me. This is not pretty from certain angles, but it beats walking downstairs.

After we exchanged a few pleasantries, I turned to go back into the house and nearly walked through the glass of the sliding door which - I realized with a sinking sensation in my gut - seemed to be stuck. Several good tugs told me it wasn't stuck - it was solidly locked. A few rational, highly analytical thoughts rushed through my keen mind, like: "What the hell's going on"? "Who did that"? "Now what"? etc. I had no idea how it happened. It had never happened before. I didn't see any hovering UFOs, but it certainly seemed like the act of a hostile alien.

What's the big deal, you might ask, unless you know about my deck - the smaller one, with no access to the ground. Still, a healthy, agile young fellow should have no trouble climbing down the ten feet or so to terra firma. Just so. But unfortunately none of those three adjectives describes me at the present stage of my career. They all applied to me at one time of course, but arthritic hip joints have stolen a step or two from the lightning speed of my youth. The situation is further complicated by the realization that I am not as svelte as I once was; in fact, rotund is the applicable euphemism for my present profile if you must know.

So the problem was clear. I was stuck outside on the deck, and even with the moderate temperature I would not remain comfortable for long, dressed, as I was, for indoors by the wood stove. And I couldn't expect anyone to arrive home for at least four hours. Can hypothermia be four hours away? I had no tools. The deck furniture was in hibernation. The dog was inside looking out at me with a silly expression on her face, either laughing or drooling or both. It was obvious that she wouldn't be of any help.

After about a half-hour of tugging and banging on the incalcitrant slider, the idea slowly infiltrated my mind that I would not get in the house from the deck. That left only one way out of the dilemma; I would have to figure out a way to get down to the ground. I pictured myself hanging at arms length from the edge and finally letting go, only to land with a sickening thud, transplanting what was left of my hip joints up into my shoulders. Or landing with a sharp crack, as my femur shattered. Either way, I would then lie on the cold, damp ground - in the shade no doubt - until my wife arrived several hours later to find my frozen remains just a few feet from the door. If only I had a ladder. Suddenly, to the accompaniment of light bulbs flashing in my head, I had it! The tree! I would climb down the cedar that grew next to the deck and I would live happily ever after.

The first obstacle, of course, was the railing around the deck. I was a bit too bulky to fit though the gap in the rails, and I was a bit too immobile to climb over the top of the railing. But I was not too stupid to kick the middle railing off, providing instant access to the tree - which suddenly looked anorexic and unlikely to hold my weight. Why hadn't I fertilized it faithfully every year? But there was no turning back, and - muttering a few lines from Joyce Kilmer's poem - I nestled myself into her branches and began easing myself down toward Mother Earth.

Halfway down the tree I began to realize how much trouble I would be in if our neighborhood bear just happened along, rubbing a winter's sleep from his eyes and with mating on his mind. And he spots this great furry creature descending gracefully through the branches. The experts say a human can't outrun a bear, but this could be my day to set a world record. Fortunately, my descent was uneventful and I was soon safely on the ground. I had even planned ahead enough to hang my cane from the edge of the deck so I could reach it from above or below. I glanced furtively about to make sure no one had chanced by to witness the great escape, an event that, to another human, might have resembled a whale climbing down a cliff to get to the beach.

But I wasn't in from the cold yet. Reflecting on all those dead bolts and security chains we'd installed, I contemplated the tightly locked house. There was no way in, short of shattering some window glass. And those double-pane windows would cost a king's ransom to replace. But with a flash of genius I remembered that my wife probably left the door from the garage to the house unlocked, so if I could get into the garage I was as good as in. The only choice was to break one of the oversized panes in the overhead door and squirm through the opening. The good news was that the opening would accommodate my bulk; the bad news was that it was four feet off the ground. But after locating a concrete block to stand on and after breaking the glass and carefully removing the fragments from the frame, I was ready to forge ahead.

A head-first plunge through the window frame was the only workable approach, and I would have to hope I could catch myself on the lawn tractor once inside. Again, it wasn't pretty - but it worked, leaving me with only a few bruises, pains, and aching joints. An hour and a half had passed since I innocently stepped out onto the deck. Luckily, I had kept so busy my body temperature drop was limited to a mere ten degrees. And luckily, once inside I had an ample supply of an old Kentucky remedy on hand to ward off illnesses and evil spirits and to thaw me out and restore essential functions such as a heartbeat. And - luckily again - no one passed by to witness the spectacle of a pair of heavy-duty, polar fleece-clad legs waving from the middle of the garage door before disappearing into the darkened cavern. Home at last.

The End

A Grave in Ballintemple

3

A Grave in Ballintemple

The quiet village of Dundrum lies about 10 miles west of the famous Rock of Cashel in County Tipperary. The countryside around Dundrum is lush and green, with rolling hills much like the Berkshires of Western Massachusetts. Long ago, my Mother spent the first eighteen years of her life in this very village with her two brothers and six sisters. Many years ago, I paid a brief visit to Dundrum with my Mother and one of those sisters. They were able to point out the house they had lived in, the church they had walked three miles to attend, and the railway station where they had boarded the train to start their voyage to a new land so many years ago. Beyond that they seemed to remember very little - not surprising since they had left Ireland almost 60 years earlier. The departure of the English family from Dundrum followed the premature death of my Grandfather Christopher English who, with lungs weakened by tuberculosis, did not survive the influenza epidemic of 1919. One or two at a time, six of his nine children and their Mother followed that time-honored tradition of the Irish seeking a better life and set out to cross the westward ocean for America. By then one of the brothers and two of the sisters had married and begun their adult lives in other counties of Ireland. So by 1924, Dundrum had seen the last of the Englishes.

I had, of course, never met my Grandfather, but I carry his first name, Christopher, as my middle name which, I suppose, inspired some extra sense of kinship with him. Somehow, through all the years I had preserved a small photograph of him inherited from my Grandmother who had lived with us all my life until her death when I was 21. His photo, together with one of her, still sat on my bedroom dresser. Christopher English was an exceptionally handsome man from all reports and the photo bears that out. He held what would have been a good, steady job in rural Ireland in those days and the photo shows him in his postman's uniform on his rounds.

Through a quirk of fate, I recently found myself in Dundrum with three or four hours to spare. On a quick tour of Ireland, my traveling companions had decided to spend a Sunday afternoon golfing at the Dundrum golf club. A bum hip has forced me to abandon such activities so, after depositing the golfers at the caddie shack, I drove about the Irish countryside of my ancestors thinking I would do a little searching for my roots. Although I have been in Ireland often enough, it seemed there was never time for exploring the back roads much less the graveyards. But in the last few years I have developed a strong interest in my Irish roots - on both my Mother's and my Father's side - and I was eager to take home some tidbits of information.

The first surprise of the day popped up as I wandered casually along a leafy, unpaved country lane not far from the County Tipperary village of Dundrum. There were no signs whatsoever indicating that any form of life had ever passed through the area, save for the road builders. My road with no name all at once intersected an identical thoroughfare clearly marked with a green street sign just like the one marking any street in the U.S., but this one read, in large white letters, "Henneberry Cross". Did someone bearing my family name own property near this spot at sometime in history?

Henneberry Cross sits about 40 miles as the crow flies from the Henneberry family farm in the little County Waterford town of Ardmore, yet I am sure that no Henneberry living there was aware of the landmark. On the other hand I am sure that my Mother, growing up about a mile away, must have passed this way many times. It would have been impossible to miss the sign but it would have held no significance for her then. What would she have said if she had be able to foresee the major role the name Henneberry would play in her life, even to its becoming her own name and that of her children.

Back to my wanderings. I had never heard anyone mention the grave they had left my Grandfather English behind in so many years before, but it seemed a reasonable goal to seek in the few hours available to me. After all, where would one be buried who lived and died in a rural village? Not too far away I reasoned, and off I went to find someone who could point me in the right direction.

My first stop was the Catholic Church in the crossroads of Knockavilla, a few miles down the road from Dundrum. I knew my Mother and her family attended Mass there regularly; she herself had showed me the row they always occupied where she and her sister/best friend Mary often brought down their Mother's displeasure for giggling during the sermon. But there was no one to be found on my Sunday afternoon visit, and I was surprised to find that only priests were buried in the small graveyard behind the church. I next tried St. Mary's Church in the village of Dundrum proper, but I soon learned that it was Church of Ireland and I am sure no relatives of mine were members there.

That particular Sunday afternoon in Dundrum was a very quiet one, attributable no doubt to the fact that the Irish Derby (Darby to them) from Curragh racecourse near Dublin would soon be telecast, to be followed by a World Cup football match (a soccer game to us Yanks). As I cruised the short street that is the village, I noticed "Bertie's Pub" at the end of my Mother's block. A conversation in a pub might turn up some clues, I thought. A knock brought no response, but as I turned to leave a fellow came across the road on a direct path to Bertie's door. As we nodded greetings I decided to take a chance and pose a question. It was taking a chance because the briefest question asked of a rural Irishman can lead to an answer long enough to exhaust a mule's ears while failing to convey any of the information one had hoped to gain.

"Excuse me sir, but may I ask you a question?" was the simple beginning. "Certainly, certainly, certainly." answered my man, Joseph Buckley of Dundrum. It could be said of Mr. Buckley that he had a tendency to repeat himself. It could even be said, not unkindly, that he repeated himself repeatedly. Which was probably just as well since he had a brogue thicker than overcooked oatmeal and I needed at least three chances to catch what he was saying. "Would you tell me" I began - at the risk of sounding like a man posing a riddle - "If a man died in Dundrum 75 or 80 years ago where would he likely be buried?"

Mr. Buckley rummaged and mumbled over my question for a while as he passed the time tamping, lighting, and relighting his pipe. But finally he said (several times) "Ballintemple's the place, for sure" and he assured me (repeatedly) that he was definitely my man because it just so happened that he was employed by the Graves Commission and spent two days a week at Ballintemple. I told him it would be worth a few pints to me if he could spare the time to take me to Ballintemple Cemetery which, I had learned from him by then, was just a few miles out of the village. Not trusting the long-winded directions one inevitably gets in rural Ireland, I thought I could save some time if my man led the way. He suggested we fortify ourselves for the journey with one of Bertie's pints and immediately the door to the pub opened as if by magic in response to a wave of Mr. Buckley's hand.

Bertie's Pub, which could not be accused of being too up-scale, held a handful of early afternoon patrons all of whom gave me a polite, if somewhat disinterested, greeting as Mr. Buckley introduced "his friend from America" all around. I have concluded that, despite the great Irish hospitality we have all heard about and I have experienced in other settings, strangers are looked upon with some suspicion in "local" pubs. But in "Bertie's Pub" in Dundrum I was largely ignored as the wagering went down for the preliminary horse races at Curragh.

As I waited for the head to settle on my Guinness I reflected on the enigma that was my Mr. Buckley. He stood all of five feet two inches, including his spiffy baseball cap. He wore what appeared to be an Irish Hurling club shirt, bright green and yellow and sporting a large advertisement for Harp beer, which gave him a rather common appearance. But then I noted that under the colorful jersey he wore a starched and ironed striped dress shirt and a respectable necktie. Based on my well-known foolish optimism and on his repeated assurance that "Joseph Buckley is a decent man", I decided to place my trust in him and off we went in quest of Ballintemple; I had nothing to lose but a few hours time.

The old cemetery was exactly where my man had said it would be and it took all of 5 minutes to drive there from the center of the village. It occupies a square of ground several hundred feet on each side and it is entirely surrounded by a wall about four feet high. There are spectacular views to the south and east, but not a sign of life in any direction. A large crucifix with a life- size image of Christ guards the gates of the graveyard, as it does in all the cemeteries I have seen in

Ireland, and the grass was clipped and neat. Twenty years ago the graveyards of Ireland were a national disgrace, but an effort was mounted about that time to clean them up and the change is now noticeable all over the island. Ballintemple is a good example of a little money wisely spent.

As my new friend and I approached the main gate, we intercepted a woman as she was leaving the cemetery. She was nicely dressed and I took her to be about my own age. She and Mr. Buckley appeared to recognize each other in a vague way and we all proceeded to introduce ourselves. We found we were speaking with one Mary Farrell née Ryan, widow of Francis Farrell of Dundrum - gone these 20 long years. Mrs. Farrell had just finished placing some flowers on her husband's grave and "had tidied up a bit" she told us. I commented on the fact that my Grandfather's sister Molly had married a Ryan and we had cousins named Ryan in America who originated in this area. We also learned that Mary Farrell's Mother's maiden name was Dwyer while my Grandmothers's maiden name was O'Dwyer. I guess we are all related if we go back far enough.

It seemed unlikely that Mrs. Farrell would remember anything about a family that had left her village before she was born, but I asked her anyway if she had heard of the English family in Dundrum years ago. She had not, she said, but after a few moments' careful thought she added "but I am sure there are some Englishes buried here down in the corner". So she led the way.

I was not expecting any surprises as we walked through Ballintemple, the three of us chatting as we went along.

Following Mrs. Farrell's example we stopped near the southeast corner of the cemetery and, as we continued our conversation, I looked down at the gravestone sitting right at my feet. It was the first gravestone I had looked at in Ireland. It is a simple grey stone with the inscription "Christopher English, d. 1919". After investing less than an hour of my time and the cost of two pints of Guinness in my search for Irish roots, I was standing on my Grandfather's grave. Somehow, I knew he wouldn't mind.

The End

The Little Yellow Bird

4

The Little Yellow Bird

My Mother was born in rural Ireland as one of seven sisters, five of whom eventually emigrated to America. The English sisters of Dundrum, County Tipperary also had two brothers, with one of them leading the way to America while the other remained in Ireland for life. Mother lived to a ripe old age and still had all her faculties, reading large-print books until she died at 98; the six of the sisters who have died so far averaged 95.5 years of life. It seems there are some pretty good genes in the family. Mother's youngest sister, known to one-and-all as Aunt Monica, is alive and kicking and, at age 97 as this is written, has already extended the family average. Which brings to mind a long and convoluted story.

In 2001, in response to the events of September 11 of that year, the FAA, rather chaotically at first, broadened the scope of the Temporary Flight Restriction or TFR. Suddenly, large areas of restricted airspace would pop up and pilots, with very little notice, scrambled to keep clear of them. As fate would have it, we were in the air over New Jersey in our Flying Club's Cessna 172 when the first of the new-style TFRs was announced. Air Traffic Controllers had no more warning than pilots did and confusion reigned supreme that first afternoon. By now you are asking what all this has to do with Aunt Monica.

During Mother's 96th year, while we were living on South Street in Pittsfield, she decided she would like to invite her sister Monica, then 88, for a visit. Since we had more space than we knew what to do with in our large and gracious colonial, this seemed like a good idea. It also seemed like a good occasion to make use of the Cessna, so, knowing that Aunt Monica - despite her age - would go for the idea, I started planning the flight and watching the weather forecasts.

At the time, my aging Aunt lived in Brielle on the Jersey shore not too far south of Asbury Park; the nearest airport was Monmouth Executive, not far from the coast. She made arrangements to get to the airport, we set up the time and date, and then we all sat back to see what the weather man would bring us that day.

My VFR flight plan called for us to fly directly from Pittsfield to Middletown, New York where we would ask New York Approach for clearance to transition New York airspace. Then we would turn south and, with the air traffic controller looking over our shoulder, fly directly to Freehold, New

Jersey, staying well to the west of Newark to avoid the congested New York area. At Freehold, a sharp turn east would put us on the last, short leg to Monmouth Executive. I figured about two hours for the trip, depending on the winds.

The weather on the appointed morning was good in Pittsfield and the forecast was fairly promising along our route. It was one of those days where you really had to go take a look at the weather before finalizing the go/no go decision and so we did. With my wife Pat as my navigator, we climbed out of Pittsfield and by the time we were over Copake Lake we could see a large cloud bank over Connecticut and some doubt was cast on the wisdom of the trip. But things looked better to the west, so we climbed to 6,500 ft to avoid some scattered clouds and by the time we reached Middletown the sky was clear.

New York area Air Traffic Controllers have the reputation of being an impatient bunch who don't suffer fools gladly, but let me say up front that the controllers I dealt with on this day - or any other day for that matter - were consummate professionals, several of whom did way more than they were required to do to assist me safely though the chaos soon to break loose and to ensure that I didn't bust any FAA regulations - which were changing by the minute it seemed. So what happened?

On June 16, 2003, Orange, New Jersey was honored by a Presidential visit when George W. Bush visited the city as part of an initiative to highlight the importance of small businesses to community development. Unfortunately, that was the day we set out for Monmouth. Still very much in overreaction-mode after the events of 9-11, the FAA modified the old TFR rules and created a giant restricted zone centered on Orange and extending close to 60 miles in every direction. The trouble was they announced it and implemented it simultaneously, with scrambled explanations of what was expected of everyone involved and practically no notice to anyone - controllers and pilots alike were tossed into a cauldron of confusion.

Back to our story. With clearance granted by New York Approach, we turned south over Middletown and anticipated an easy flight to Freehold and on to Monmouth Executive - but it was not to be. Suddenly we received a radio call from Air Traffic Control instructing us to turn right immediately to a heading of 270 degrees and to fly clear of the restricted zone. A brief description of a brand-new TFR followed, together with the promise of more instructions to be relayed soon.

An impromptu revision of our flight plan had us fly west nearly to Allentown, Pennsylvania to make sure we cleared the poorly-defined TFR. The controller, admitting that no one in his shop had a clear idea of what was going on, stayed with us despite an obviously heavy work load. By the time we had circled south and were passing over Princeton he approved a left turn and an approach to Monmouth Executive. That approval didn't last long. He was back a few minutes later with instructions for a turn to the South. We would not be allowed to land at Monmouth after all because it was within the forbidden zone of the TFR and no one could enter without a "special clearance".

A major complication was that he had no idea where we could get such a clearance, but he suggested we continue to fly south and contact Atlantic City Approach; maybe they could provide the needed special permission. We changed frequencies and asked Atlantic City for a special clearance to fly to Monmouth but the controller had no idea what were talking about. By the time we switched back to New York the news was better: we could land at Monmouth after all since it wasn't really inside the TFR; our earlier instructions were in error. It was clear the controllers we talked with were embarrassed by the confusion and at the same time angry with the system that generated it. Fortunately for pilots in the air, they came down on our side and provided all the help they could.

Turning around and heading back toward our destination we realized our next challenge would be the weather. Unexpectedly, the turbulence had increased and the ceiling became lower and lower as we approached Monmouth until we were forced to descend to 2,000 ft; that was as low as I was willing to go considering my unfamiliarity with the area and the possibility of tall, uncharted obstacles. Pilots call this "scud running" and most are well aware of the risks involved. Fortunately, we soon had the airport in sight and before we knew it we were touching down on runway 14. While I headed for the fuel pumps Pat went into the small terminal to locate Aunt Monica - who was probably getting a little anxious wondering why we were an hour late.

Our passenger was ready and waiting and excited by what she called the "big adventure". This was her first flight in a small plane and she was raring to go in what she called "the little yellow bird". Pat and I had been concerned about our 88 year-old Aunt being able to climb up and fold herself into the back seat of the little Cessna, so we had brought along a small, folding ladder to help her along. We needn't have worried; Aunt Monica waved off the ladder and hopped into the back seat as quick as you please.

My Aunt is well known to be a prodigious talker, but with several radio channels to monitor in congested airspace we had to put a gentle lid on it. As we fitted her out with a headset and explained how to use the push-to-talk button we stressed the fact that we needed her to keep silent except when we called her or if she saw other aircraft coming near us. She caught on to this idea right away and stuck to the rule all the way.

After checking with Allentown Approach again and heading east over northern New Jersey we encountered a low-hanging cloud layer, but with an updated weather report for the Berkshires showing clear skies we climbed to 7,500 feet putting the cloud layer below us and clear, sunny skies above us. There is an ethereal sense to hanging above the clouds in a little airplane, seemingly motionless; it was clear Aunt Monica was mesmerized with it all and her eyes, compromised vision and all, never left her window. Near Philmont, NY we descended through a large hole in the clouds and soon found the promised clear skies as we approached the rim of the Berkshires. Despite all the diversions, delays and frustrations we completed our projected four hour round trip in less than six hours of flying time.

Mother welcomed her guest warmly as Pat went right to work in the best Irish tradition - getting some heat under the tea kettle. There was no shortage of conversational topics and the evening went quickly. Aunt Monica bubbled over with excitement about her trip in "the little yellow bird"; her enthusiasm persists to this day; forever more she has referred to her trip as "the flight of her life". Clearly, the return trip to New Jersey would not be by car; in her mind we were already locked into the idea of taking her home in that same little bird when the time came.

Shortly before bedtime, Aunt Monica announced that she would like to go to Mass the next morning. Pat said there was a 9:00 AM Mass at St Theresa's every day; "it's not far away and I can drive you there tomorrow". The next morning, Aunt Monica insisted she wanted to walk back to our house after Mass. She was used to walking about a mile every day and didn't want to stop getting her exercise. The church and our house were less than a mile apart and right on the same street so the idea seemed reasonable enough.

10:00 AM came and went and Pat realized we should have seen Aunt Monica by then. A quick look up the street toward the church didn't reveal any walkers heading our way, so Pat's next move was to call the secretary at St. Teresa's to see if anyone had seen our missing church-goer. Their report was that several staffers had noticed her at Mass and seen her leave, heading in the right direction, more than half an hour ago. By the time Pat searched most of the way to the church and back with no results, Aunt Monica was more than an hour overdue and we were getting more concerned by the minute.

When Pat had inquired about Aunt Monica at the church, Sister Teresa, the Pastor's assistant, was in the office and, on her own initiative, took off on a search up and down the nearby side streets. Sister Teresa had often brought Communion to Mother at our home and was a favorite of the family, but her search was fruitless that day.

Meanwhile, Aunt Monica, spiritually refreshed and enjoying a brilliant Berkshire morning, set off from St. Theresa's on a leisurely stroll back to our house on South Street. After a while she came to a steep hill she didn't remember, but soon she was on the level again and, although her vision was not great, she thought she was passing the Country Club across the street. Another few hundred yards and she came to the Berkshire Life building which she recognized as the place Mother had worked for many years and the place her Godson (me) had "helped build" as a laborer for the Gilbane construction company in 1958. Although Aunt Monica had visited Pittsfield many times in the previous 50 years she had never driven a car so she didn't have a strong sense for exactly where things were located; she had no idea she had passed our house before she started up that steep hill.

By then Pat and I were getting pretty worried (we hadn't told Mother that anything was amiss). It was hard to imagine what had become of our 88 year-old Aunt, but it was clearly time to involve the Pittsfield Police department in the search. Within minutes, a patrol car staffed by a sympathetic young officer arrived, gathered the information, and took off on a search of her own. We were afraid to leave home in case Aunt Monica showed up so we stayed near the phone with an eye on the driveway.

Meanwhile, our "missing person" continued what she still considered her morning walk home from Mass. Being in excellent shape for an elderly woman she didn't notice any extra level of exertion, although by the time she reached the bottom of "snake hill" just south of Berkshire Life she had already walked well over a mile. Before she went too far up the long, curving hill, our delinquent walker began to realize something was wrong but, not realizing she had gone too far, she continued up the steepening grade. It was time to ask for some directions. Finally, as she arrived at the entrance to the South Mountain Concert Hall, she spied a Verizon crew hard at work and, catching her breath, she headed their way. Recognizing that this "older" woman was somewhat distressed, the two young linemen interrupted their work to listen to her story. She had by then walked close to two miles up a pair of steep hills on a hot morning and she was beginning to show the effects.

It must be said that Aunt Monica, at this stage of her life, tended to rattle on in a stream of consciousness Joyce would have envied. In the best of circumstances it was difficult for even those who knew her well to follow what we might politely call her verbal wanderings. The lineman gave each other perplexed glances after a few minutes of listening. This woman, who had arrived in this remote spot on foot, was relating the strange story of how "she was trying to find her nephew's house because he had brought her up from New Jersey above the clouds yesterday in his little yellow bird to visit his Mother and his wife had dropped her off at church and she was afraid everyone would start worrying about her especially if she was late for lunch and she was feeling very thirsty just then and ...."

The Verizon men concluded they had an elderly nutcase on their hands and knew they had to humor her while they figured out what to do about the situation. After finding some water for their visitor, they decided to call 911. The Police had by then put a few more resources into the search and were quick to respond to the phone call from the Verizon guys.

Once Aunt Monica thanked her rescuers and was settled into the Police cruiser, our favorite young policewoman, having already been to our house, knew just where to deliver her passenger - which was fortunate since Aunt Monica could not remember our address. A happy reunion was held in our driveway a few minutes later, and before long we were all gathered over a cup of tea to hear the details of the great adventure. Although everything turned out all right and we could have a good laugh over it now, it was easy to imagine a number of things that could have gone seriously wrong and might have had dire consequences. Obviously, some new rules were going to have to go into effect at our house so that anyone over 80 would not be allowed to go walking alone. Fortunately, not too old to have learned a little lesson, Aunt Monica herself suggested she probably shouldn't go walking by herself until she got to know the neighborhood a little better. We all agreed on that.

Pat and I expressed our thanks to the Pittsfield Police Department which had responded immediately and never took the situation lightly. The Officer we dealt with could not have been more understanding. We also felt we should show our gratitude to the Verizon crew members who stepped right up to help out. By coincidence, our son Rich was then a

Verizon executive in the District of Columbia office. We relayed the story to him and he recommended our heroes for a Company award; a photo of the two lineman receiving the award appeared in the Verizon Newsletter a few weeks later along with the story of the lost lady.

Several weeks later it was time for Aunt Monica to go home to Brielle, but by then the TFR was history and the weather cooperated with a bright, clear day. This time we filed a flight plan that would take us right over Newark Airport and give us some great views on our way. From 3,500 ft over Newark we looked straight down on several dozen brightly-colored airliners scurrying around on the taxiways and taking off and landing at regular intervals. But the most spectacular view of all was the New York City skyline from Yonkers all the way south to Battery Park and beyond to the Statue of Liberty. After overflying Newark we crossed Raritan Bay with Sandy Hook well to our left, and headed straight into Monmouth Executive. Our turn-around and the trip home went just as smoothly.

Our passenger was reluctant to see the end of her "great adventure" and probably knew there would be no more chances for her to travel in "the little yellow bird". She never tired of telling the story; a few people we know may have tired of hearing about it, however. I myself had feedback from more relatives than I needed to hear from. I especially didn't need to hear from the ones who gave me a hard time for putting such an elderly woman in such grave risk by squeezing her into the back seat of a tiny airplane. No sense arguing with them.

Aunt Monica thanked us for her trip repeatedly for many years, but the best thanks was the look on her face as she stared out the window of N-12477 while we cruised over her adopted land. I would have given a lot more than a penny for her thoughts just then.

The End

Liam's Kettle

5

*Liam's Kettle**

I blame the whole thing on our daughter Ellen. If she and Ben hadn't decided to move to Oregon last year no such thing would have happened. If she had stayed here in the East, our first grandchild would have been born right down the road and his Grandmother would not have had to fly one-eighth of the way around the world to wash his diapers. Then we would still have our old tea kettle and we would have saved all this time and trouble.

As winter faded and spring showed signs of arriving on schedule in Oregon, so did Liam. Ellen and her Mother, who seldom talk on the telephone more than 26 hours a week, began to increase both the frequency and duration of their calls. If I had any money left after paying the phone bill I'd buy AT&T stock. I think this form of behavior is related to our dog's sudden interest in the puppy nest I'd made her as whelping time grew near.

As Ellen's magic moment approached, her Mother, Pat, began to panic and started calling travel agents in the middle of the night. Suddenly she announced she had booked a flight to

Eugene at a bargain price, also known as a king's ransom. Fortunately, it was on a scheduled airline and daylight travel was permitted; unfortunately, her itinerary included most major U.S. cities and the trip would take one full day.

So the race was on between the arrival of the baby who came to be known as Liam and the arrival of the special day on which Pat could fly west so long as she didn't leave on Wednesday but definitely stayed over Saturday. Fortunately, Liam won. Unfortunately, he won by a little too much and Pat didn't get to Oregon until he was almost three weeks old. But the delay served a purpose of its own because by the time Pat arrived Liam had learned how to really make her feel needed by expressing - on an hourly basis - the only bodily function he had yet mastered.

The problem with all this was that it required leaving me at home alone, something which is rarely permitted to happen due to my documented inability to function independently in a domestic setting. Whereupon who rushed to the rescue but my Mother, volunteering her services as a foreman of the one-dog ranch for the duration of Pat's absence.

Stepping briskly into the breach with her 84 years of experience, Mother knew just when to tell me to eat my dinner, take out the garbage, and change my socks. In fact, she made sure all of those items were placed before me in the proper sequence, avoiding potential disaster. I, in turn, still had a warm and lighted home to return to each evening, and all was well in the Berkshires. At least it was until I turned my back on the tea kettle a moment too long, giving the demonic electric range a welcomed chance to melt the kettle to a blob of metal and plastic.

The solution to the problem seemed obvious. Get a new kettle identical to the old one and Pat, on her return, would never be the wiser. So off I went to the nearest purveyor of common kettles. But life is never that simple. Four shops later and it was clear that the style in tea kettles had been revolutionized since the last late and lamented kettle had entered our home. That evening I was forced to report my failure to Mother, who had somehow, after only twenty-four hours, grown tired of boiling water in a pot. Off again the next day, my marching orders were to try a few other emporia but to be prepared to settle for a different design; we could not, after all, have Pat come home to a kettle-less house. But - I was warned - whatever I do, don't get a whistling kettle.

It must be said in our defense that in a thoroughly Irish household, few possessions play a more central role than the tea kettle. The unscheduled arrival of a guest, a telegram, a letter from across the great pond - or I think even a stray goat - demanded the immediate application of heat to a full kettle. I'm sure the first phrase I ever uttered was "I'll put the kettle on". To merely contemplate a home without a proper kettle was to confess to great shame, for how could one be properly hospitable without one? So the quest for "Liam's Kettle" became the obsession of the few days left to me before my wife's return.

At this point I must admit that the "great kettle meltdown" was less than a complete disaster for me. Actually, I had always hated that kettle. Its sophisticated design - based on the exact science of human ergonomics, I suppose - directed all the steam right at my hand every time I tried to pour from the stupid thing. Even worse, it had the disturbing habit of letting its handle fall with a sharp report whenever I least expected it - usually just as I brought cup to lip for the first sip of boiling-hot tea. So the idea of searching for a kettle of a different design had a certain attraction for me.

Soon I had haunted all the local kettle shops so frequently I was drawing strange glances; rumors abounded that there was a mysterious "kettle pervert" loose in the city. And I knew all there was to know about every kettle in town, from color to capacity. But the search for the perfect kettle was fruitless; either they were whistlers or were equipped with the confounded "falling handle" or were too small or were the wrong color. So as Reggie did 2597 times before me, I struck out.

Pat returned in an air of euphoria from her first visit with number one grandson. If silver prices rose during her visit to Oregon, it was due solely to the sudden increase in film sales; the suitcase that held the teddy bear on the way West returned full of photos of the heir to the Throne. Applying a neat psychological touch, I casually eased the matter of the meltdown into the conversation at my first opportunity. Still at thirty thousand feet mentally, Pat took it all in stride and seemed to enjoy her tea brewed with water boiled in a pot. But the next day she was off to shop for a kettle; I told her I hadn't been able to find time to look for one.

A Daydreamer's Digest

The first candidate brought in for a trial had a pleasing shape and was the perfect size but, in its gleaming white porcelain finish, looked out of place in our earth-tones kitchen. After a brief summit meeting, votes were cast banishing candidate number one to the "returns" department. The next evening Pat proudly displayed her latest find: in stainless steel with a "defeatable" whistle, no less. And just the right size. I casually announced how stupid-looking it was with its pot shape, huge cover, tacked-on spout, and inside-out handle. Poor judgement. Off I was sent in a state of exhaustion the next day to resume my search for the perfect kettle.

The exhaustion stemmed, at least in part, from the tossing and turning during my new series of "kettle nightmares" which made its debut the previous night. But this time I strode forth with a firm chin, for I had learned a new secret. In mentioning to Mother my hatred for the kettle with the crashing handle, she pointed out that if I'd "just tighten that little screw on the handle it wouldn't fall anymore". I smartly replied: "Oh". Armed with this new gem of knowledge, and with the exact location of every kettle in twelve shops burnished into my memory, I marched briskly into my favorite discount store and grabbed the red one. It was exactly like the old one, handle, spout, color and all. I felt as though I had come home from a long voyage in a strange land! Mother tightened the little screw on the handle and it hasn't fallen yet.

The End

*Originally published in *The Berkshire Review*, 1995.

The Santa Virus

6

The Santa Virus

Within a few weeks in the spring of 1993, in the Four Corners of the southwest - the only place in the United States where four states share a common border - thirteen people died of a mysterious and alarming illness. After a few days of flulike symptoms, they progressed to a fatal respiratory distress syndrome. This pathology was recognized as something new by alert investigators in a New Mexico state agency and they started the ball rolling in what turned out to be a fascinating story of medical detective work at its best.

In an outstanding example of cooperation, agents of numerous state and federal agencies, working night and day and using the latest methods of modern biology, were able within one month to identify the cause of this new illness as a novel form of the Hanta virus. The deadly new disease has come to be called Hanta virus pulmonary syndrome.

Richard Henneberry

A less mysterious and far less deadly virus suddenly made its presence felt at the holiday gathering of our clan in December, 1996. Our virus resembled the Hanta virus with its flulike symptoms and events conspired to make it inevitable that we would call it "The Santa Virus" although it didn't arrive to the clatter of hoofbeats on the rooftop, and it didn't use the chimney, it was definitely lively and quick.

A lot of planning had gone into our family gathering, which would mark the first time in 5 years we were all together for Christmas. Mike and Rhonda had the short trip, just 2 hours from their new home in Weston, Connecticut; they loaded up two year old son Patrick and ten year old dog Ashley in the trusty Tahoe and headed north on Saturday morning. By that time, Kathy and Ken had the van rolling for the second day of their trip. From Gastonia, North Carolina to the Berkshires is just too much for one day - especially hauling a four year old, a set of two year old twins, and a large dog named Tia. It is only through the miracle of modern technology that such a trip can be made at all - the miracle in this case being the portable TV-VCR combo that plugs into the cigarette lighter and plays videos all day long. True, the kids begin to resemble zombies by noon but have you ever noticed how quiet zombies are?

There is also a strange effect on the parents. Until you have traveled 1,400 miles listening to the Busy Town theme song you haven't lived. But the North Carolina contingent made record time and arrived late Saturday afternoon. Meanwhile, Ellen, Ben and Liam were winging it east on Delta from Seattle after driving two hours from their home in

54

Bellingham, Washington. Their trip was uneventful, if you can live with spending the night in an airline seat the width of the average american thigh and waking to the aroma of freshly warmed peanuts served by the quarter-ounce in unopenable foil packages. Its what's for breakfast. Pat and I met the sleepy-eyed and starving cross-country fliers at Bradley Airport near Hartford, and delivered them home just ahead of a small snow storm - enabling me to keep my promise of a White Christmas for Liam.

The travelers from the other, closer Washington were last to arrive; Rich and Lisa were almost ignored as we welcomed Miles, the newest member of the family. We were relieved to see how readily this frisky four month old puppy became fast friends with his three canine cousins. So there we were, all sixteen of us plus more than 300 pounds of dogs counting the host German Shepherd, gathered under one roof, anticipating a hectic but healthy and happy holiday. Little did we know the plans the Santa virus had for us.

Later, looking back at the week's events, we reconstructed the route the Santa virus had taken in crashing our party. Attention quickly focused on the large, white-bearded gentleman seated right behind Liam on the flight from Seattle to Atlanta. This fellow had been lucky enough to find himself next to a vacant seat and had gained some degree of comfort by swinging the armrest up and spreading out a bit. He was far from completely comfortable though, nursing as he was a nasty cold with wheezing and sneezing. Liam thought he remembered hearing the old fellow mumble in his sleep something about eight reindeer and a sleigh, but Liam himself slept most of the way while the planes dry, germ-laden air was continuously recycled.

With the family all gathered at our house, Saturday went along smoothly enough. Mike, Ben and Liam sallied forth to the great woods of Canaan in quest of the tree-to-beat-all-trees. I saw them off with my usual, breathlessly-awaited fatherly advice, saying "get a tall one, its a big room". And a big one it was, fully fourteen feet to its tip. Mike and Ben were well pleased with their effort, although Liam had cautioned them "don't take a chance on that one". His words were recalled as we tried to wrestle the tree through the door. But the Christmas tree was up and decorated by the Saturday night before Christmas - early for us.

The first sign of the albatross trailing our ship appeared that evening, as Liam suddenly spiked a high fever and took to his bed. Ben was next to fall, with a reprise of Liam's symptoms. Rather than go down the roster one-by-one, suffice it to say that we fell like flies. Symptoms differed somewhat from one individual to the next, supporting some speculation that two infectious agents were loose in the household. My own view is that the Santa virus was able to do all those things by itself, affecting everyone differently. Some people were pretty sick but Liam may have been sickest of all. By Christmas Eve, as his temperature approached 105 degrees F, Ellen and Ben decided not to wait any longer for medical help and hurried off to the new Express Care Unit at the Medical Center in Pittsfield. Liam was treated swiftly and professionally and, I was happy to note, without using an antibiotic against what had all the signs of a viral infection. Physicians are finally starting to respond to the decades-old warnings from microbiologists that unnecessary use of antibiotics sets the stage for the emergence of drug-resistant bacteria. Then the antibiotics - which have no effect on viruses in any event - don't work against bacterial infections when they are needed.

Several scary new drug-resistant pathogenic bacteria have emerged in the last few years, selected for by the very drugs intended to destroy them. This remains a sensitive issue for me; In the late 1970's my own mentor, C.D. Cox, presented the keynote address at the annual national meeting of the American Society for Microbiology and spread the warning about the inevitable consequences of promiscuous use of antibiotics. So the problem is not so new as we are led to believe; the handwriting has been on the wall for more than fifty years.

Christmas morning dawned as scheduled and it seemed we were about a year away from the total chaos we might have expected from five little kids and a roomful of presents. Liam and K.G. were old enough to anticipate Santa's visit, but they hadn't counted on his virus and were too sick to be fully involved. Hannah and Nicholas were still healthy, and tried to get into the spirit of things. So did Patrick, at only 21 months, but by that time Mike and Rhonda barely had the strength left to hand him his presents. In fact, wanting only to get home and crawl in bed, Mike and Rhonda moved up their scheduled departure a couple of days and went home Christmas morning. Mike finally recovered enough to have a beer, but just one, by New Years Eve.

The turkey got off easy this year. By dinner time Christmas day we were barely able to raise a quorum. The planned sixteen for dinner had shrunken to eight, and several of those seemed to have little enthusiasm for eating. Just before dinner, I noticed that old familiar scratchy feeling in my throat but no one could accuse me of eating like a sick man. As the evening wore on, I knew I was coming down with our sneaky, uninvited guest. But, with my flu shot just a month old, I hoped for the best. Pat was also showing some symptoms by Christmas night, and by the day after Christmas our house looked like a MASH unit right after a chopper's arrival. I grabbed a clipboard and took morning report.

Mother had some heavy-duty upper respiratory symptoms by this time, and we kept a close watch on her fever. On Friday, after all our visitors had left, she visited the physician's office and had an antibiotic prescribed to ward off any secondary infections. This is an appropriate use of an antibiotic, since in an 89 year-old patient the risk of a sudden onset of a bacterial pneumonia while weakened by a viral illness is far greater than the risk of selecting for drug-resistant bacteria. We were thankful that Mother had her flu shot when Pat and I did; the Santa virus gave her a bad enough time, but it could have been lots worse. In the final analysis, 13 of the 16 members of the family succumbed to the Santa virus and 15 of the 16 showed some symptoms. By January 4, only Ken showed no signs of the illness. He not only gets a gold star for being healthy and strong, he also gets the annual award for patience for his hours on the road and for putting up with his sickly in-laws.

The Santa virus, while in no sense as serious as its rhyming relative the Hanta virus, is not to be taken lightly. The speed with which Santa's flu raced through our healthy group was remarkable, and few of us are completely recovered as I write this. The week was not a loss, although the party did not live up to expectations. Everyone was too sick to engage in arguments - always a risk when families gather but something we don't do much of any more; age mellows everyone eventually. The dogs got along famously, and Miles stole more than one heart. Miles is a breed most people don't know: a Catahoula Leopard dog. An American breed, originally from Cajun country. If he is typical, his breed deserves to be better known. Where did he get his name? Rich's favorite trumpet player, of course, the late Miles Davis.

Thursday evening was devoted to packing up for Friday morning departures, but one more bit of excitement remained. Nicholas, never known as the shy and retiring type, took a flying leap over our dog Skete only to do a face plant on the edge of the coffee table. The coffee table won the encounter, and Nick came away with a nasty gash on his upper lip. Off again to the Express care unit in Pittsfield, where a plastic surgeon was called in to place three stitches in the little guy's lip. Nick was completely recovered in about an hour, while his parents seemed to have recovered from the episode by the next day.

We were back to normal by Friday evening, if coughing, wheezing, blowing and sneezing can be considered normal. For Ellen, Ben and Liam, however, the epic journey was not over. By the time they were ready to leave our house, the major storm in the Northwest was already well known. At noon on Friday I called Delta airlines to inquire about the status of the flight to Seattle and was informed that everything looked good, no delays were expected. In fact, by this time the Seattle airport had already been closed for 24 hours. But the airlines care only about having customers in the seats if their planes are able to go, so they never warn anyone off; let the flyer beware! Predictably enough, our travelers connecting flight from Cincinnati was canceled and Delta put them up for the night at a nearby Quality Inn. They even gave them $10 each for meal money - hold that shrimp salad! But it beats trying to settle down in an airport seat for an overnight stay. Finally, our weary travelers arrived in snowbound Seattle, dug their car out of the parking lot, and spent five hours completing what is usually a two-hour drive to Bellingham. The happy ending was that they all felt much better by then, Liam was able to get out and enjoy the rare heavy snowfall in Bellingham, and their dog Gretel, still a little upset at being left out of the family gathering, was very glad to see her humans.

Within a few months we will mostly remember the pleasant moments of this year's Holiday gathering; the aches and pains will be largely forgotten. And we are thankful that all the travelers had safe trips. But next year I am going to check Santa's pack very carefully; he'll still be welcome but he can leave his virus at the North Pole where it belongs.

The End

A Moving Tale

7

*A Moving Tale**

As a displaced New Englander for almost all of my adult life, I always thought I would come back home on that far-off day when I retired. But when a promising job in my rather esoteric field unexpectedly materialized right in my old home town I could not resist. So the plan was to move the household 400 miles north to Western Massachusetts after 20 years in the Maryland suburbs of Washington, D.C.

The plan didn't include leaving our Maryland house on the market for two years while we made two mortgage payments each month, but that's the way it worked out. The "recession-proof" D.C. area housing market showed no sign of weakness until the day we listed the house with a realtor, then the bottom fell out of the housing market from San Diego to Bangor. The Laffer curve had come home to roost, and the Laff was on us.

Moving out of a house after 13 years carried some surprises, the biggest of which was that six people could accumulate so much junk in so short a time. Everyone was called upon to make some tough decisions but it was probably toughest for the senior Henneberry (me) who had to part with many of his highly valued automotive treasures - uncharitably referred to as "his old car parts" by other members of the family. After parting with numerous prizes, I finally reduced my holdings to one spare Porsche engine and transmission, an extra set of wheels, two perfectly good 911 fenders and several boxes of "previously owned" gems of German engineering. All this - plus the Troy-Built Tiller - went into the pick-up truck, which cursed softly in Japanese. After lengthy deliberations, the brain trust decided that it made the most sense to leave be-hind - temporarily - my trusty old 1968 Porsche Targa. It had recently been semi-retired to the status of summer toy and was badly in need of some heavy-duty rust repair which was not compatible with the two-house budget, so it was better off spending the duration in our Maryland garage.

Finally, the great day came - financial salvation was at hand; a buyer appeared, a mortgage was approved, and a closing date was set. I was suddenly pressed into service to retrieve the remaining belongings. Any car fanatic will immediately recognize that there was no way I could send anyone else to do this job. The Porsche and I went back 16 years; this par-ticular car actually represented the best and brightest pieces of three such specimens I had driven to the iron oxide limits over the years, each time salvaging things like fenders, seats, engines, trunk lids, and sundry bits and pieces, some of which were hybridized with the next derelict I brought home to keep me driving in style. But that is another story - this one is about moving.

I outlined what seemed like a fool-proof plan. An 18-foot truck with a car trailer was reserved through the national office of a large truck-rental firm which shall remain nameless; for crossword puzzle fans I will say the name begins with "R" and has five letters. I specified the auto trailer rather than the car-hauling dolly to minimize the trauma to the Porsche by getting all four of its wheels off the ground. I would pick up the customized rig in Maryland, proceed to the house where my son Rich would meet me to help with the loading, and I'd be off. Piece of cake.

I showed up on schedule at the rental shop, already feeling like John Candy trying to get home for Thanksgiving. It had taken a van, two trains, a subway and a taxi to deliver me - about 10 hours after leaving home - to the starting point for my return trip. This being the U.S. of A. in 1991, the proper rig did not, of course, await me; does anybody care anymore? The story was that it was the fault of the national office - they had specified the dolly, not the trailer. Strangely enough, the computer-generated bill showed a rental charge for a trailer, not a dolly. The dealer tried to convince me I would be happier with the dolly anyway; it would be easier to handle than the trailer, he promised - as he revised the bill. Being committed to a tight schedule, I decided to make the most of it and went ahead. Rich and his buddies Art and Chip had everything loaded by a little after 7 PM and I decided to get rolling right away and stop when I got tired. Rich had power-ofattorney to handle the closing on the house two days later, so there was nothing to keep me in Maryland any longer. With a watchful eye on two large, converging weather systems I sallied forth. It was Christmas week.

Sailing around Baltimore and heading north on I-95 I was feeling fine and decided to postpone my first coffee stop until the Jersey Turnpike. The weather was still holding as I came off the Delaware Memorial Bridge at about 10 PM, and everything was looking good as I eased into the tollbooth to pick up my Turnpike ticket. But my tranquil evening was suddenly shattered as the gatekeeper calmly told me I couldn't take "that thing" on the Turnpike; trailers were OK but dollies had recently been declared taboo. I argued that this decision had received less-than-nationwide publicity and it sure left me in a tough spot. He expressed his sympathy by saying "Yeah, well go past that white truck over there and get off the turnpike". No, he didn't know anything about any other routes north through New Jersey, and I'd have to get moving because the traffic was backing up behind me. As I slowly pulled out of the tollbooth, I saw two white trucks about 30 yards apart parked on the shoulder. I passed both and tried to turn off as instructed when I suddenly realized I had gone one truck too far. The turn-off was between the two trucks and there was no way to get back to it. There is no backing up a loaded car-hauling dolly - at least not with my skills - and there was no turning around with the Turnpike traffic whizzing past my shoulder.

So there I was, about 100 yards up the Turnpike without a ticket. I sat there and mentally listed my options. Even if I tried to get off at the next exit I would catch hell for not having a ticket, be thrown out into the night and then be stuck on local routes in an area completely unknown to me; it could take days to go the length of New Jersey, stopping at every stop light. Looking back at the toll booth, I couldn't tell if the attendant had noticed my failure to follow his instructions. Maybe he phoned the state police right away or maybe he just shrugged his shoulders and went back to work. Maybe he hadn't even noticed my mistake. Straight ahead was clearly the only way to go, but what would I do when it was time to get off? A little white lie about losing my ticket might work - unless my favorite attendant had sounded the alarm. What was the penalty for proceeding up the turnpike without a ticket? Was it a capital offense in New Jersey? Would they sentence me to a week in Atlantic City? When in doubt, drive on! At least as far as the first available cup of coffee.

One of the best features of New Jersey is the many service areas along the Turnpike, and I wasn't many miles from the first one. But they were long miles, suffering as I was from a bad case of feeling conspicuous. Why wouldn't I feel that way driving a big yellow truck and towing a bright red Porsche on - God forbid - a dreaded dolly. And not knowing if there was an all-points bulletin out for me, the infamous Turnpike Cheater. As I signaled for the turn into the service area I smiled as a late model, bright red Porsche Targa went flying by with a cheerful toot of his horn and an insouciant wave of his whale tail. I saw him signal for the service area as he rapidly grew smaller in the distance; although I had only about a half-mile to go to the exit, I figured he'd be finishing his coffee before I got there to order mine. Thinking of the pile of bucks it takes to purchase one of those rockets I figured the driver was some city-slicker, maybe a banker who had emptied out one of the S & Ls while Ronnie's "regulators" were looking the other way. Occasionally, I am wrong when I leap to such conclusions; I was completely wrong about this guy.

Four hours of bouncing along in one of Ford's finest rental-fleet trucks had a salubrious effect on my bladder, so my first goal in the service area was the gentlemen's lounge. Mission accomplished, I stepped into line for coffee right behind the only other customer in the place, who quickly deduced that I must be the clown towing the old Porsche through the storm-threatened night, and I realized he must be the guy driving the red whale tail. Before I knew it he was buying me a cup of coffee and we sat down to compare notes. It was immediately clear to me that this guy was no dilettante, but rather a true aficionado of the great German auto marque and a man who came by his cars honestly. In fact, my new-found friend was Peter himself, proprietor of Peter's Foreign Car Service in East Orange, New Jersey.

The conversation soon turned to my current dilemma, and suddenly I didn't feel quite so alone. Peter's attitude was that anyone towing one of these relics through a mid-Atlantic winter's night must be a true believer and therefore deserving of whatever help could be given. Within minutes, he had worked out a plan: he would give me his turnpike ticket and I would drive the length of the Turnpike, adhering to the speed limit, straight to the exit to connect with Route 17 near the Meadowlands. If Smokey stopped me along the way I should play dumb, show him my ticket, and suggest he must be looking for someone else. Once there, I would bluff my way through the tollbooth saying that was the ticket the attendant gave me when I got on and nobody said anything about my dolly. Meanwhile, when it came time for him to get off the Turnpike, Peter would claim to have lost his ticket. The worst they would do was charge him the full toll from start to finish of the road and he was going almost the full length of it anyway.

Let me make it clear that I am seldom accused of being the shy and retiring type. I have no doubt that I would have - alone over coffee - formulated a plan and muddled through. This was definitely not one of life's great challenges confronting me, but it was certainly a major aggravation and I could feel my irritation rising with the truck rental people and the State of New Jersey and I knew it must somehow be all Dan Quayle's fault. Also, though I am not especially superstitious or excessively religious, the fact is that Peter had roared out of the darkness in his red 911 by some strange coincidence just as I was badly in need of some help. And it was Christmas week.

Peter's plan worked to perfection. I saw a few patrol cars but they showed no interest in me as I motored along trying to look as innocent as a guy from Peoria driving a brown Chevrolet sedan. I had to suppress a smile when the toll booth attendant apologized that "They gave you the wrong ticket - this is for a car and I've got to charge you the rate for a truck with a trailer". I felt obliged to feign a brief argument for appearances sake, but in truth I would gladly have coughed up a few hundred bucks in tolls at that point. I now had a simple

Richard Henneberry

shot up Route 17 to connect with the New York Thruway and another 3 hours from there to my driveway.

The weather closed in just about the time I entered New York State, and my 3 hour timetable went south. As I approached the ticket booth for the New York Thruway I didn't know what to expect. Were dollies of the car-hauling type welcome on this highway? I got my answer in the form of a cheerfully delivered Thruway ticket with no questions asked. Strangely enough I had reason to retrace this route early the following month and encountered some equally bad weather; as I approached the same entrance of the Thruway I noticed the flashing sign: "Nothing in Tow" But there was no such sign in December when I showed up in a big yellow truck with a dolly in tow, and I motored on into the snowy night.

It wasn't a trip I am eager to repeat, mostly due to a few more malfunctions of my ill-prepared truck which showed up when the going got tough. Way back at the beginning of the trip I had found that the takeup reel on the driver's side seat belt was malfunctioning; the belt hung loosely in front of me most of the trip but I was lucky enough never to put it to the test.

Halfway home I found that the windshield washers didn't work - no fluid would spray no matter what I did. Not a problem when the pavement was dry and not an issue while the heavy snow was falling. But about halfway up the Thruway the snow stopped and I found myself traveling a slush-covered highway. A stop for a jug of fluid to fill the reservoir didn't solve the problem. By then I had stopped at

70

every rest area and service area along the Thruway, but never for long. I didn't dare nap with the engine running and with the outside temperature about 12 degrees the cab cooled in about 15 minutes. Finally, with the traffic picking up as the longhaul truckers emerged from their late-night roosts, I was blinded by the spray from every passing truck and I realized I would just have to park 'till sunrise.

Dawn wasn't too long in coming and on arrival it did let me see the road so on I went, taking the Berkshire spur of the Thruway from a point about 8 miles south of Albany and traveling about 40 miles East to our home right smack on the NewYork-Massachusetts border. I pulled into the driveway at 7 AM, twenty-four hours after leaving home and twelve hours after waving goodbye to Rich in Maryland. Not bad time considering that the one-way trip takes a heavy-footed driver about 6 hours in a fast car equipped with a good radar detector.

Awakening in my own bed later that day, the 24 hour round trip to Maryland seemed more like something I had dreamed than something I had just completed. But a glance out the window showed the yellow truck and the red Porsche in the driveway and I remembered a promise I had made myself sometime during the previous night. Going to the phone, I dialed the number Peter had given me for his shop in New Jersey.

Richard Henneberry

I told myself I was just calling him to report my success and to thank him one more time for his help; but a little voice inside me insisted the call was motivated as much by my need to confirm that my Jersey Samaritan really existed. After all, it was Christmas week.

The End

* Originally published in *european car magazine,* 1993

The Birthday Dinner

8

The Birthday Dinner

Mother started celebrating birthday number eighty-nine a few days early with a 4th of July gathering at our house, attracting partygoers from as far away as Connecticut, North Carolina, and the District of Columbia. The darkness of the daylong downpour was brightened by the four great-grandchildren to be bounced on the knee, by the gourmet dinner prepared by her granddaughters, and by the antics of the three dogs commissioned as groundskeepers for the day. Although the birthday was four days away, the party was a great success.

Continuing what Mother considered a weeklong celebration, my sister Anne planned a quiet dinner at her home in Galway, New York for the 6th of the month. Not overlooking the always-necessary potatoes, Anne focused her attention on the salmon fillet carefully chosen for the occasion. And cooked to perfection it was, flaking away at the touch of a fork and thoroughly enjoyed by all those present. Or so it seemed.

After dinner, never the one to interrupt the pleasure of post-prandial relaxation and the quiet of an evening, Mother chose to keep a small secret from the rest of the household. It seems a remnant of the salmon's skeleton had taken up residence in her throat, lodged beyond the reach of a finger and undisturbed by the swallowing of bread. It can be confidently stated that the particular salmon Anne had invited for dinner had no intentions of ending up this way, even to the extent of a single bone.

Before being selected by my sister in her favorite fish emporium, this particular anadromous fish had already traveled nearly half the world by sea and air. (Anadromous is a fine example of the big words scientists love to use; in its defense, it is from the Greek meaning "running upward" and it aptly describes the salmon's upstream trip to spawn. And it is spelled correctly, in case you wondered). Mother's salmon was a Pacific salmon, a member of the genus *Salmo*. Atlantic salmon are technically not salmon at all but are members of the trout family in the genus *Onchorhynchus*.

The basic difference between Atlantic and Pacific salmon, other than their home port, is in their spawning habits. Pacific salmon spawn only once, then die; Atlantic salmon can spawn several times. And it is true, salmon do return to their birthplace to lay their eggs - as many as 7,000 at once. As they reach the fingerling stage in their development, the next generation of salmon may begin their migration downstream to the sea, although they are generally a year old before setting off on their ocean odyssey - which can cover several thousand miles. Scientists have several hypotheses to explain how salmon, without the help of AAA or a phone call home for directions, can find their way back to the exact place they hatched; some think they navigate by the stars, others think they store the taste or the smell of their birthplace and follow it back. There are fewer hypotheses about the cause of a salmon's death after spawning, a phenomenon reminiscent of a flower having to die to spread its seed. In any event, this particular salmon met her destiny in a net off the coast of the Pacific northwest and was - as are most "fresh" fish today - quick frozen for a fast trip east and her rendezvous with Mother's esophagus.

Mother suffered in silence until late Sunday morning. Then, realizing the problem wasn't going away by itself, she finally confessed her secret to Anne and Dave and they were soon off to the nearby medical clinic. The clinic appears to have a policy that all patients will wait three hours before being seen. They are really doing patients a favor with this apparently heartless policy since the patients will be so exhausted from waiting that the shock won't register when they learn the cost of the visit. Concerned about federal laws that might prohibit any special concessions for Mother's advanced age, the staff decided she should wait the full three hours before the promised X-ray was taken.

We all talk this way. We say we are looking at an X-ray when, in fact, we are looking at the photographic record it leaves behind. The X-ray itself, of course, is invisible to the human eye and only exists for that brief moment while the technician is hiding in the other room leaving us to wonder just how safe this stuff really is. But the X-ray leaves a record on the film just like light leaves a record on our Instamatic film, and we look at the film and say we are looking at the X-ray.

We all know that the film looks like a negative rather than a print. But when Mother's X-ray was pronounced negative it meant that it revealed nothing out of the ordinary, so she was sent home and told to forget about it - "maybe you have a little cold". Mother, of course, knew someone was missing something but, as usual, she didn't want to make a fuss. Anne had long since left for the office and Dave was ready to go for another week of workaday bliss when the buzz of the telephone grabbed his attention. The caller quickly explained that a more thorough reading of the X-ray had indeed revealed the presence of a foreign object in Mother's throat and she should proceed directly to the doctor's office. They should have let Mother read the X-ray in the first place; she knew where to look!

The rush to the doctor's office in Troy was, of course, followed by the mandatory three-hour wait in the comfort of the modern molded-plastic chairs with all the softness of a slab of slate. Fortunately, there was a pile of 8-month-old magazines provided to help pass the time. Finally, the brief examination confirmed the presence of a sizable foreign object lodged firmly in Mother's throat. Its removal would require anesthesia best done in a hospital, but she was promised she would only be there overnight - just as a precaution. So Dave aimed his impromptu ambulance at Samaritan Hospital in Troy, where Mother was welcomed like an old friend though this was her first visit. She was admitted as an inpatient, a process that includes at least a hundred questions. When asked if she would like a telephone by her bed, Mother paraphrased a Hal Roach joke in replying, "Oh no! I won't be here long enough. One way or the other, I'm out of here in the morning". Next stop was radiology for more X-rays, on to the laboratory to have blood drawn, then the history and physical. Mother said she was so tired from all the tests she was looking forward to some rest under anesthesia - to sleep, perchance to dream! Her procedure was scheduled for 7:00 PM Monday evening July 8, 1996 her 89th birthday!

Shortly before he convinced himself that the sun - not the earth - was the center of the universe, Copernicus had discovered Murphy's Law; it applies today as it did four hundred years ago. It applied with full force that Monday evening in the operating room as Mother waited, and waited, and waited to be wheeled in. So many delays occurred that before she knew it she had fulfilled her mandatory three-hour wait and was on her way, leaving the nervous relatives in the comfort of the waiting room to entertain themselves with hilarious sit-com reruns on TV. Mother's procedure was serious enough in itself and everything is a little more serious when the patient is 89 years old. And Murphy himself seemed to be lurking around that operating room! But this time we had only a short wait. We were all much relieved when Dr. Sherr delivered a three-inch salmon bone which he described as one of the largest he had ever extracted. Mother bounced back immediately from the light dose of the newest intravenous anesthetic, spared by scientific progress from all the nausea and discomfort that used to characterize recovery from the old inhaled-gas anesthetics. And the tasty anadromous fish, in the end, caused lasting harm to no one.

Declaring the whole deal a piece of cake, Mother was ready to go home at morning's first light. She found a night in the hospital a mysterious thing, with plenty of time to ponder the reasons why so much effort is spent in preventing patients from sleeping. Nevertheless, the sun finally rose and we were there by 9 AM, ready to take the patient home. But had we forgotten something? Of course, the cursed mandatory three-hour wait! Promptly at noon one of the physicians from Dr. Sherr's office showed up to sign the release form. Mother stole a line from another famous American as we pulled away from the hospital door: "Free at last, free at last, thank God almighty we are free at last".

The End

The '94 Season

9

The '94 Season

Memories of my grammar school days in the 1940s still rattle around in my mind. Strangely enough, the events of the summer of 1994 suddenly brought several of those memories back into focus. Unless you are old enough to remember, you may be surprised to learn that those early years of the cold war were fraught with fear. There was scarcely a body on the planet who did not have an image of the great mushroom-shaped cloud burnished on his or her soul, and as charter members of the nuclear age we watched the rules being written - we didn't know what to expect.

This uncertainty bred some strange behavior - mostly the behavior of grown-ups that scared the hell out of kids. Even as fourth graders we didn't gain much confidence from starting off every school day with a drill to see how fast we could scramble into the security of that great air raid shelter under our desk. We were well-practiced in identifying the air raid siren and knew just what to do when we heard it. We were also well-rehearsed in exactly what to do if we were to see a blinding flash of light and we knew how fast we'd better do it. The Nuns at St. Joseph's would not have cared for the boys' jokes about that drill, alluding as they did to a certain unmentionable anatomical location and a sentimental farewell.

A few years later and Civil Defense was all the rage. As I recall, this consisted mostly of men in tin hats storing empty, olive-green, five-gallon cans with yellow triangles painted on them; these mostly went in basement stairwells of schools and other public buildings. The plan, as best my young mind could grasp, was to fill these with water at the sight of the first bomb; I guess the rationale was that it's best to keep busy while you wait to be vaporized. And of course fallout was a big issue; the prosperous among us were advised to store enough canned food and water in our basements to last a few months - unless we were truly prosperous and could build and stock a proper fallout shelter. And of course we were too polite to mention the question of human waste - which might have become a bit of a problem by the second month with the whole family cooped up in the basement.

Two particular days from those long-ago grammar school years stand out in my mind. On the first day I am an eleven year old boy standing in the schoolyard looking up at the biggest manmade thing I have ever seen aside from the Empire State Building. Its huge wings each carry three giant engines with the propellers pointing backward spewing six sharp contrails against a pure blue Berkshire sky - yes, six engines. And yes, all propellers at that point in its existence; jet engines were added later, believe it or not. But this is our firsthand introduction to the realities of post-war life - one of the first B-36s out of Westover AFB some 40 miles to the East, still climbing but low enough to be seen in detail - silver with hatched cockpit windows way out in front. The impression is still with me, but it defies analysis. All-in-all, I think that B-36 was for me more a symbol of security than of anxiety but I know that wasn't true for all my schoolmates. Did that B-36 have anything to do with my five Air Force years to come later?

The '40s were not known as the decade of sensitivity, of course, but in retrospect it seems grown-ups back then must have assumed that children had the mental skills of gerbils - except we had never heard of gerbils at the time. How many children of the '40s carry scars from the scares of those days to this day? More than a few, I can tell you. I guess we were just supposed to take it all in stride, to feel that these were natural events - this scrambling under desk tops and listening for sirens and digging shelters and stashing empty water cans. In fact, I can tell you now, most guys laughed at all this stuff. We were smart enough to know what the mysterious atom bomb and the even worse hydrogen bomb could do - we had seen newspaper pictures and newsreels at the movie theater. And we also knew that if such weapons started falling on us our school desks were not going to offer much protection and we would not be around long enough to get too thirsty for the water we had yet to put in the olive-green cans.

Many of my peers still carry excess baggage from those days, more often the girls than the boys. I came through with few, if any, scars - I think partly because boys were more likely to hide their insecurities behind jokes about such scary things. That's how the psychologists explain it anyway, making little of the fact that humor can have great value in defusing tension and can contribute in a major way to sound mental health. But there was another facet to my surviving the fears thrust upon us in my youth. I had an anchor of my own, a personal port in a storm; I had something more important to worry about - Baseball! The Season! The Pennant! The World Series! The Yankees!

Western Massachusetts is as close to New York as to Boston and there were nearly as many Yankee fans as Red Sox fans in the Berkshires in those days and whichever team you chose you could get your nose broken for it in my schoolyard. But our family's roots were in New York so the Yankees were "my team" from birth. "Break up the Yankees" was a cry I knew only too well, but nobody did and they kept on winning until I was no longer a lad.

The other memorable day from my youth brought back to me by recent events happened late in the summer of '50. As a 13 year old faced with the threat of soon returning for yet another year of terminal boredom in the classroom, one of my great pleasures was to spread a blanket outside the dining room window near the cherry tree, to run an extension cord out the window for my ancient Philco portable, and to tune into Mel Allen's broadcast of the Yankees game - sponsored I think by Ballantine beer in those days.

This particular day stands out in my mind for more than one reason: the Yankees, Red Sox, and Tigers are all in the race as

September draws near; the Yankees' remarkable rookie has earned a place on the pitching staff; and the world is in a turmoil with places with funny names like Seoul and Pork Chop Hill in the news every day. Looking back from almost fifty years later I now know the Yankees would go on to capture the pennant and embarrass the Whiz Kids from Philadelphia in four straight in the series. And I know the rookie would win ten games that year and stick around long enough to become Whitey Ford, the winningest Yankee pitcher of all. And now I know that the "police action" in Korea would be just the first of many burrs under our national saddle, and things would never be the same again.

But with that day in my mind I can feel the warmth of the late summer sun and I can remember the thoughts that wouldn't go away: why can't everybody stop these wars and throw away their nuclear bombs and why can't everyone stay healthy and why can't everything stay just the way it has always been. After all, there is an important pennant race in full swing and the Yankees are in the thick of things well into August and I'm only 13 years old and I want everything to stay this way forever. I hear Mel Allen - sorry, the mellifluous voice of Mel Allen - as the rookie Ford is brought on in relief in a tense situation. And the innocence of my youth is preserved for at least a little longer as the game goes on.

The game does not go on any more. In 1994, the remarkable rapacity of the owners collided head on with the amazing avarice of the players and one of the best seasons of recent years was suddenly history. The Yankees are back on top after many years of wandering in the wilderness, Mattingly may play in a post-season game after all, and Jimmy Key brings back memories of Whitey when the chips are down - but that's history now. Encouraged by a congress incapable of passing anything but kidney stones and pay raises for itself, baseball remains exempt from the laws that govern other businesses. The owners, having conveniently shed themselves of the encumbrances that come with having a commissioner, put one of their own in his place and continue to strain our credulity by crying poor. The players, many of them spoiled kids who have had their own way too long, fake some negotiations but mostly go golfing with total indifference to the common folks whose livelihood depends on the game.

There would be no World Series in 1994. Mattingly would never have the chance to emulate Mr. October. Paul O'Neil would not take his hot bat to the fall classic. Jimmy Key would not win 20 games. Fans in other towns have their own litanies of sorrow and Tony Gwynn must cry himself to sleep each night. And any records that went in the books will need those famous asterisks.

The people who park the cars, and sell the hot dogs, and peddle the ice-cold beer have gone home, stopping off at the unemployment office on their way. The souvenir vendors have packed up their dated wares, not sure what will become of them. The bars outside the downtown ballparks try to hang on but there are no customers and everyday the conversation is the same. Baseball's front offices decimate their staffs with layoffs, sending many more "middle managers" out on the street. Meanwhile, the owners drool over the tax write-offs this year's losses will bring and buy lunch for their CPAs, the players bank large chunks from the emergency strike fund, huddle with their accountants about income averaging, and shop for more sports cars and gold chains. And the fans - who cares about the fans?

But maybe the fans will have the last laugh. In many towns, they discover there is a minor league ballclub and they go to a game to find the action little different from the majors; it is, after all, a kids' game. They find they can take the whole family to the game, park free in the same hemisphere, sit close enough to see faces to go with the numbers, eat hot dogs and peanuts, and have change left from a twenty. Sure, almost all the minor league players belong to the same major league owners - but do we need those players? From the fans' point of view these could just as well be town teams. That's how it all started out. And there will be no shortage of players - just give the young ones a chance to play.

We have bought the notion of the rare talents major leaguers bring to their game, and of course there is some truth in that. But there are some hints that maybe a lot of today's major-leaguers have not spent enough time playing ball. Sure, they came up through all the leagues - Little League, Babe Ruth League, Pony League etc. - leagues invented by adults for whatever reason, but they didn't head for the nearest park every summer morning to bat 27 times or to handle 30 grounders or judge 20 fly balls before lunch. And have we not seen the modern major league equivalent of Babe Hermann have one bounce off the top of his head as he circled under the "routine fly"? Sure, we had 3 Dodgers on the same base once long ago, but isn't there a little too much bizarre base running in the majors lately? And don't we see other hints that many of today's players lack a thorough understanding of their sport - like charging the mound after being hit by the pitch that forces in the tying run? Maybe these big-leaguers are not as indispensable as they think they are.

In some towns there is a sudden surge of interest in girls' softball or the over-40 men's slow pitch league. The fans are rediscovering the game itself and finding it is the game - not the trappings of the major league version of the game - that they have in their blood. Many baseball-lovers have, over the years, slowly become disenchanted with the greed that permeates major league baseball. Maybe the major league game has finally cut its own throat. Before the summer of 1994 it would have been unthinkable to contemplate interfering with organized baseball's nearly century-long traditions - to abruptly end the season in August? To cancel the World Series? But the deed is done. Baseball as we know it may not be coming back. And, hard as it is to see the old traditions die, maybe a fresh start would not be all bad.

The End

Author's note, added July 31, 2012: This article was written in 1994. As you may have noticed, my predictions have not come true. Greed still rules. Owners cling to their special exemption from the rules of commerce and pocket great profits. Players turn down $20 million per year contracts and hold out for even more money saying they have to consider the future for their families. Tickets for a de-

cent seat at Yankee stadium start at more than $200 and the best seats are over $2,000 - yet the fans keep coming, even when times are tough. We are told that major league baseball is healthier than ever. So far this season attendance is up more than 8% over last year. Reminds me of the "bread and circuses" designed to distract the Romans from their real problems just before the decline of the Empire.

The End

A Biologist's Journal: Twins

10

A Biologist's Journal: Twins

A few positive things happen to most of us as we age, and one of them is the arrival of grandchildren. In my experience, we look at our grandchildren in an entirely different light than the one in which we looked at our own children. We treat them differently too. After watching me spend time with their children, all my children agreed that "this is not the same man who was my father!". They are right, of course. The man who was their father was young, ambitious, and impatient with life; the man who is their children's grandfather is not so young, not so ambitious, not so impatient. Maybe not yet a wise man, but wiser than he was.

We change throughout our lives, but never do we change so rapidly as we do in our first few years. Like all new parents I marveled long ago at our new babies' tiny fingernails and what perfect miniatures they were. Lately, I marvel at each new milestone in a grandchild's development. I am not yet fully qualified as an expert in grandfathering, but with grandchild number six on the way I can claim some experience. And recently a whole new and unexpected element was introduced - twins!

Twins occur once in every 80 to 90 pregnancies and about two thirds of them are dizygotic - that is, nonidentical or fraternal - which happens when two separate zygotes are formed from the fertilization of separate öocytes, or eggs, by separate sperm, and each zygote gives rise, eventually, to a fetus. So the pair may be of the same gender or of different genders, and they are no more alike genetically than siblings born at different times. Occurrence of twins appears to run in some families, but only for nonidentical twins; maybe there are genetic influences on the likelihood that two öocytes will be available for fertilization at one time. Also, the frequency of nonidentical twins increases with the age of the mother. Probably, hormonal changes, influenced by both inheritance and age, are involved; maybe if I delved deeply into the scientific literature on the subject I would find lots to read and to learn from.

Monozygotic or identical twins occur for entirely different reasons; in this case a single öocyte is fertilized and begins to multiply, but early in the multicellular phase - for unknown reasons - the mass of cells divides into two primitive embryos. Remarkably, both embryos mature into complete fetuses with no missing parts. Occurrence of identical twins appears to be more a random event, not subject to genetic influence. Both twins have the same complement of genes and so are of the same gender and are very similar in appearance.

Any physical differences between them at birth are caused by slight differences in their environment in the womb. Differences occurring between identical twins later in life are the topic of perennial controversy; the nature - nurture argument is not settled yet, although clearly both can play a role. A topic for another day.

My daughter's twins are boy and girl - not identical. So we know they came about by an improbable accident; two öocytes happened to mature in the same cycle and were fertilized independently, somehow managing to survive and develop. I marvel at the consequences of this accident, caused by who-knows-what; my daughter and son-in-law can only groan when I joke about this accident giving them two for the price of one.

Hannah and Nicholas are not exact replicas of each other in appearance or in their approach to life, but they were already good friends at birth, aware of each others moods and attitudes it seems. It defies what we think we know about infants to watch the twins play with each other at nine months old; one grabs a toy from the other and both giggle loudly about it; then the other grabs it back and the giggling starts all over. It would be interesting to know if any age-matched pair of infants will play this way, or does it only happen with infants who have shared the same womb.

Watching the differences in motor development between the two womb-mates is equally fascinating. At nine months, hand-eye coordination is well developed in both; each one picks up anything reachable and brings it straight to the mouth. But otherwise, they are off on totally different approaches to life.

Hannah, sporting a constant smile, is content to sit and enjoy her surroundings; occasionally, the need to crawl around a little comes over her and off she goes. Nicholas, born a few minutes later and a few ounces lighter, is a different story. His overriding curiosity about the world around him compelled him to set off on all fours at six months. Soon, he was pulling himself upright at every chance, and - at nine months - was an accomplished, self-taught walker with the mission of checking out everything on his ever-increasing horizons. So now I marvel as I observe my grandchildren diverge from their similarities at birth and start along their separate pathways to childhood, and as I reflect on the billions of signals racing around in those little brains I am overwhelmed by the complexity of it all.

Neurobiologists believe that the number of neurons in the brain during development in utero reaches a peak and then is gradually reduced before birth; during this early period the surviving newborn neurons migrate to the regions they are destined to occupy in the adult brain, guided by a complex array of factors. Once in place, they begin to reach out to their target cells - some quite distant - to establish that magical wiring network that will eventually constitute a human mind. After birth, this processes is repeated with respect to synapses, the connections between neurons and their targets where information is passed along; a vast excess of synapses is formed by age two, then declines sharply over the next few years.

The sharp decrease in the number of synapses in brain development is probably a use-'em or lose-'em phenomenon. Axons, the long processes neurons send out to carry nerve impulses, extend along defined pathways as they seek out their targets, guided by several classes of small molecules; if they find the right target - which in the brain is another neuron - a synapse is established and the target cell will send back a survival-promoting message to the first neuron. If an axon is not successful in receiving or following the molecular cues that lead to synapse formation, that neuron dies. In this way, the vast network of synapses in the brain - something like a million billion synapses - becomes established and the basic wiring diagram of the human brain is laid down. And if you think about it, this approach to the development of the brain has an enormous implication: every brain will be different! Even the brains of identical twins. Or the brains of cloned sheep. Because the final wiring diagram of the brain in all its details is not specified by genes alone.

It seems likely that the number of synapses surviving into adulthood reflects the amount of stimulation starting at birth or even before. There is a popular notion circulating these days that reading to an unborn infant will have positive effects on its intellectual development. I would not be surprised to learn that it does just that, but I would be cautious about the inferences I would draw from the results. A mother-to-be who invests substantial time and effort in reading to her unborn baby will probably not emerge from the experience unchanged; she might, for instance, be more likely to continue the habit after the baby is born. And if stimulation in the womb improves a baby's intellectual prospects, might not twins - who presumably stimulate each other in utero - have better prospects than babies who spend their first nine months alone. The maximum level of synaptic activity at age two, mentioned above, may have something to do with the stage described as the "terrible twos" which most mothers know only too well. Will maximal stimulation at this stage of development lead to greater intellectual powers later in life, or will it lead to persistent over-excitation expressed as hyperactivity? Who knows for sure?

In this decade alone - the Decade of the Brain, so decreed by Congress - we have made great strides toward the goal many have described as unattainable - the understanding of the human mind. We are not at the point of understanding the mind, but at least we can now think about approaching that point.

Perhaps the most important thing we have learned is that we must make whatever investment it takes to complete our understanding of this process; not only will we then have achieved the greatest accomplishment of the human mind: the understanding of itself - but only then will we have the knowledge we need to nurture normal development and eliminate harmful influences from the environment of the child, to deal with the aberrations of the mind that torture so many of all ages, and to treat - or even prevent - the devastating diseases of the aging mind that are, in so many cases, the reward for survival into old age.

The End

Gus, A Berkshire Bear

11

Gus, A Berkshire Bear

Chapter I: Gus's Ramblings

Gus loved to ramble along the Taconic Ridge on a hot summer day like today. August was Gus's favorite month; he loved its long, hot, lazy days when he had nothing better to do than hike at a leisurely pace to the top of the ridge behind the Shaker Village. When he reached the top he always headed south, keeping the spectacular view of upstate New York to his right. When he first started out there were a few spots where he had a clear view to the east too, and as he ambled along he could see Richmond Pond and beyond to Osceda Mountain. He almost always veered off a little for a quick dip in a small pond near Perry's Peak. Then, as he continued south he could see Queechy Lake shimmering below him and off in the distance the Helderberg mountains near Albany were clearly visible too.

Bears don't have very good eyesight, but Gus didn't know that and he enjoyed his sightseeing tours. The view from the ridge always reminded him of that song he heard on a camper's radio about seeing forever on a clear day. And this day was so clear he could see all the way to where the earth curved away.

Gus loved August alright, and one reason he loved it so much was that so many of his favorite treats ripened at this time of year. Gus could eat his weight in berries every day and with different varieties ripening one after the other he was never far from his next snack.

As usual, Gus daydreamed as he walked. This time the dream involved not just food but some new things too, as we shall see. Here on the western rim of the Berkshires there were berries galore, including the blueberries he favored. If he had his way, Gus would go blueberrying every day of the year - but that wouldn't work, of course, because those little morsels were ripe for only a few weeks each summer. He loved blueberries the most not just for their taste, but also because he could sprawl right out among the bushes and fill right up on the succulent purple morsels without moving anything but his arm.

Being a black bear, Gus was happy eating many different kinds of food, depending on what was available. He ate skunk cabbage and grasses in the spring, berries and fruit in the summer, and acorns and beechnuts in the fall and, of course, apples. He would eat the meat of dead animals too, if he had to. And of course, like all bears, Gus loved honey, and he knew where all the beekeepers along his route kept their hives. He also knew he was not very popular with the beekeepers; more than one of them had taken a shot at him.

In the winter, Gus didn't eat anything at all. He settled into his den in early November and pretty much stayed put until early April. He would laugh whenever he overheard humans argue about whether or not black bears hibernate. All he knew was that his heart rate and body temperature drop while he sleeps through the winter months, which seemed pretty much like hibernating to Gus. And he would loose a lot of weight over the winter, weight he enjoyed putting back on in the spring. But it is also true that he would wake up if he was disturbed during those winter months, which was probably the kind of thing that contributed to the debate over whether or not he was really hibernating.

In any event, on this particular August day, after eating his fill of blueberries, Gus decided to stretch out for a nap right there in his favorite berry patch. With his tummy full of blueberries and the hot August sun beating down on him, in no time at all he was sound asleep.

Gus had always been a dreamer. Every time he fell asleep, even just for a nap, he had a dream. Not the same dream every time, but the same theme every dream and the theme was food. Not the same kind of food every time either. Sometimes Gus dreamed about his favorite blueberry patch but there was no sense dreaming that dream this time because that was where he really was and that was where he would be when he woke up. So as he dozed off his mind summoned another dream. It turned out to be a new dream that Gus had never dreamed before. As we shall see.

In this dream, Gus was a little cub again, lying lazily in his Mother's den while she chatted away with some other female black bears from the neighborhood. Unlike male bears who range far and wide, females stay much closer to their dens, especially when they have cubs to look after. And now and then some of the female bears would visit each other in their dens so their cubs could play together - and, of course, so the mothers could keep up with all the gossip. Although humans never seem to realize it, bears keep up with what is going on among all the creatures in their areas, including the humans. And although it may seem strange to us, bears find humans to be very funny creatures indeed. Sometimes they could be dangerous, but usually they were just plain funny.

Gus had heard some of the funny stories from his father and his grandfather and remembered laughing so hard he rolled around on the floor as he listened to stories like the tale of the hunter who parked his truck aiming down the hill so it wouldn't get stuck in the mud, but then it rained and the truck got stuck anyway. So this brilliant human got out and pushed on the back of the truck until it came unstuck. Of course it then took off without a driver down the hill with the hunter running in slow motion through the mud and yelling frantically at the truck to stop. The truck, of course, ignored all instructions and continued until it plunged through the hedgerow and the wire fence into Fowler's creek. Stories like that one struck bears as very funny, especially since they never bothered with things like trucks anyway but walked everywhere they went.

Hunters, of course, were not always funny; they could be very dangerous, and every bear learned that from an early age. Bears are taught to be very cautious when humans are nearby. Ever since he could remember, Gus had known about the stories of hunters sending packs of dogs into the woods to run bears down, then shooting the bears at close range when they were cornered. The humans called this sport, but bears were hard pressed to find anything sporting about it. So bears, who can move swiftly and silently through the forest despite their bulk, are very cautious when people are around.

From his earliest days, Gus had heard stories going all the way back to when the settlers first came to this part of the country. There were many tales about the great bear massacre of 1790 when the settlers, having survived a long cold winter in the Berkshires, realized they could make some very warm clothing from a bear's fur coat and so they began to consider bears fair game. In this dream, Gus listened as his Mother repeated to her neighbors the old stories she had heard from her Father and Grandfather. Lying comfortably in their den, Gus learned that he was one of a long line of black bears who had, for hundreds of years, made their home along the New York - Massachusetts border. This was a part of the world that had been largely passed by when the rest of the Northeast was invaded by the settlers. The Berkshires was rough country, with mountains and plateaus and heavy forests, so the settlers heading west found it easier to follow the rivers and valleys that bypassed the Berkshires rather than to climb up into what was obviously unfriendly territory. The Indians, like the bears, had lived quietly in the Berkshires since time began, walking quietly on the land. They held bears in high regard and were no threat to Gus's ancestors. In fact, in some Native American cultures bears were considered to be Gods, which struck Gus as pretty funny.

As the hunters arrived, the mighty animals drifted north and the bear population dwindled in the Berkshires. But in recent years it was the human population that had dwindled to the point that by the time Gus became an adult there were only about 130,000 humans left in all of its 1,000 square miles and almost all of them were clustered in a few cities and towns. Many of the laboriously-cleared fields returned to forest as farm after farm closed down, and these second-growth forests were friendlier to bears than the original New England forest with its tall trees and largely brush-free forest floors. Now there were plenty of hedge rows and bushes loaded with all the things bears liked best. The bear population was making a comeback.

Black bears tend to be nocturnal if there are too many people around but not many humans lived in Gus's area and he rarely came face-to-face with one. Gus had heard all the cautions about steering clear of humans, but he couldn't help being a little bit curious about what they were really like. Eastern black bear males like Gus could cover a range of 120 square miles every day in the summer, just ambling along scouting for food.

By the time Gus was just 3 years old he was fully grown and had roamed all over the Berkshires from Mt. Greylock in the north to Mt Washington in the south, and from the Taconic Ridge in the west to the Berkshire Barrier in the east. But Gus grew up on the Taconic Ridge and called it home. As fate would have it, our house is situated about a quarter of a mile from the top of that same ridge.

Chapter II: The Bear Ran Up the Mountain

Summer days in the Berkshires can be spectacular, and today was one of the better examples. Marveling at the warmth that lingered into evening, my wife Pat and I relaxed on the deck. Skete, our faithful, four year-old German Shepherd, was on guard duty at our feet. From our vantage point we could keep a close watch on the hummingbird feeder about 15 feet away at the corner of the deck, but we couldn't see the bird feeder around the corner. This spring was an exceptional one for the varieties of birds visiting our feeder; the most colorful of our guests this year included rose-breasted grosbeaks, rufous-sided towhees, American redstarts, indigo buntings, and several varieties of finches. But the hummingbirds were out in full force this early summer evening and we were content to watch their spats over access to the feeder and their flying practice featuring endless lazy-eights and high-speed spot landings on tiny branches.

As the mystery writers always say, the tranquility of the summer evening was suddenly shattered - not by a gunshot

109

or a crash of thunder - but by an outburst from Skete; she can move with lightening quickness when she wants to, as anyone who has played ball with her can testify. On this occasion she was on her feet and around the corner before I could stand up. I followed her angry bark but by the time I turned the corner she had disappeared, still barking, into the dense woods. I could hear clearly the breaking of branches and other sounds of crashing about. Luckily, Skete responded to a few sharp commands to come and reappeared in a moment or two. Meanwhile, I was slowly assembling the pieces of the scene before me into a sensible picture.

The first image processed in my visual cortex was the bird feeder pole bent to the ground *sans* bird feeder. And there on the ground some 15 feet from the pole was the bird feeder on a direct line with the point at which our visitor, with plenty of encouragement from Skete, had disappeared into the woods. Skete stood beside me vociferously expressing her eagerness to return to the chase, and the noises which could only represent a large body moving quickly through the thick brush could still be heard. It didn't take the skills of Inspector Maigret to deduce what had happened. Clearly, our resident black bear had been interrupted in the process of procuring an evening snack. At Skete's urging, the bear ran up the mountain.

The presence of a black bear in our neighborhood had been well known for at least five years, although only a few of our neighbors had caught sight of him. He was seen carrying a garbage pail out of a neighbor's garage several years ago, and our nearest neighbor actually photographed the furry creature a few years earlier as he drained her bird feeder. And just a month ago Pat and Skete, on a morning trip down the long driveway to fetch the newspaper, had come face to face with the burly bruin. As dog and human froze in a mixture of fear and fascination, the visitor gave a loud snuffle and took his leisurely departure.

The Eastern black bear has become quite common in the Berkshires in recent years, and he has appeared in more than a few back yards. So far there are no reports of his physically tangling with humans in this area, although there have been a few reports of overzealous officials destroying black bears they perceived to be a threat. There have been recent reports of black bears wreaking havoc with campers in the west, even reports of attacks on campers and hikers. But that is a different animal - not the Eastern black bear.

Many of us accustomed to the sight of deer, fox, and turkey still find something special about meeting a bear in the wild. Bears seem to be of special interest to us, maybe because they are so like ourselves, walking about on their hind legs, making loud noises, and eating constantly. Or maybe it's because, of all those creatures from the stories of our childhood, bears come closest to living up to our image of them when we finally meet. But thanks to Skete this is the story of one bear who got caught with his hand in the honey jar and didn't get away with the goods.

Another week went by and our furry guest was back, this time for a more leisurely visit. Again Skete saw him first, and stood in the kitchen barking at him frantically through the glass of the side door. But this bear obviously knows about doors, and he continued to demolish the new birdfeeder pole and went to work on the feeder itself. Through it all, Mother - well over 80 by this time - sat nonchalantly on the front deck; at first she wondered why I was getting so bossy when I invited her to hurry inside through the front door around the corner and out of sight of the visitor. But soon we were all assembled at the window watching this magnificent creature no more than 20 feet away as he shattered the birdfeeder in his powerful jaws until he could drain the seeds into his mouth. When I stepped out on the deck for a better look, he gave me a quick glance and casually wandered off down toward the pond. I fumed over the fact that my camera, for the first time in more than twenty years, was in the repair shop. The bear's visit went unrecorded.

Chapter III: August's Berries

A few more weeks went by before the big fellow decided to present us with another photo opportunity, and this time he stayed a while. The good news was that my camera had arrived back from the repair shop the previous day; the bad news was that I hadn't gotten around to loading it with film yet. But this bear was determined to pose for some photos that day, so he stuck around while I got ready. It was during this visit that we decided that such a frequent visitor deserved to have a name, so we called him "August" for the month he arrived; by some stroke of luck we had happened on the same name his mother had decided on. And, being Americans, we had to have a nick-name for our new friend, so naturally we started calling him Gus.

Finally, I stepped out onto the side deck with a loaded camera while Gus, still about 20 feet away, glanced at me briefly and went right back to consuming his red berries. He had bent a tall spicebush to the ground and sat on his haunches happily filling his face. The trunk of the tall bush lay horizontally between Gus and me; it probably gave me a false sense of security, and since Gus gave no sign of considering me a threat, I moved forward slowly, hoping for the best possible photo shot.

Sitting there with what appeared to be a big smile on his face, Gus looked a lot like a slightly larger version of our German Shepherd except for his teddy bear ears. He showed no signs of being a threat to me and he didn't seem to care at all that I was there. He might have changed his mind if I had reached for any of his berries, but I kept both hands on the camera. In any event, Gus suddenly decided to provide me with my surprise of the month. He slowly rose to a standing position and looked right at me. Just when I thought he had reached his full height he continued to rise taller and taller until I was face-to-face with a beautiful, black giant of an animal standing at least 7 feet tall. I was too busy shooting frame after frame on the SLR to be scared, although I must confess to a little case of shaking hands after Gus ambled away. I would like to report that he waved goodbye, but that was probably my imagination.

It seemed like forever before the prints came back from the photo studio, but when they did I was relieved to see I had some great shots. I think one of those photos of Gus standing by his bush is, all things considered, my favorite among all the pictures I ever took before or since. In the photos it was clear that Gus's right arm was damaged. In the excitement of the moment of photographing the berry feast I had the fleeting thought that his arm was bent at the wrist and that he wasn't using it normally. I again had the sense that his arm had been injured as he sauntered down toward the pond clearly using only three of his limbs and keeping the right arm tucked up out of trouble. The photos confirmed the injury.

Several weeks later, after all the excitement died down, we learned that an oversized black bear had been captured in our vicinity. Apparently, there had been reports of the big fella tangling with a moving train and so the authorities decided to bring him in and see what they could do for him. I was gratified to learn that my estimates of Gus's size - widely disbelieved - were confirmed. In captivity Gus weighed in at 430 lbs and was estimated to have a standing height about the same as Wilt Chamberlain - well over seven feet. Most black bears in the northeast are much smaller - under six feet tall and weighing about 200-250 lbs. But Gus was not truly oversized for his species; Eastern black bears weighing over 800 lbs have been captured from North Carolina to Canada. The North Carolina guy holds the eastern black bear record of 880 lbs. No one recorded how many berries he could consume in one day.

In captivity, Gus had found the right hosts: after setting his broken wrist and giving him a month or so to recuperate, they released him several hundred miles to the northwest in the wilds of the Adirondacks. While I am sure Gus is still enjoying his daily summer strolls along some spectacular mountain ridges and finding more berries than even he can consume, I know how far guys like him can range and I always keep my eyes peeled in case he stops by Canaan for another visit. And I always keep film in my camera.

The End

Over the River ....

12

Over the River....

When Mom told me we were going to visit Nan and Pop's house for Christmas, she did what she always does. She sang me a song about it. It was a new song for me, but how many songs does a guy know when he has only been around for a little more than a year?

The new song was all about traveling Over the River and Through the Woods to get to my grandparents house and the trip sounded like it would be fun. I figured we would proba- bly drive the car to the train station, then take a nice train ride for an hour or so till we were near Nan and Pop's place, then - from all the things Mom sang about in my new song - we would probably have to ride on the sled behind the horse to get the restof the way to the house. It sounded as though it might get a little cold behind the horse, especially if he kicks up some snow, but then we'd go into the nice warm house with a fire roaring in the fireplace and be warm and cozy in a hurry. What did I know?

I remember being at Nan and Pop's place at least once before, but my memories are a little fuzzy. The last time we were there I remember there were lots of people around and then these guys came and put up this great big tent in the yard. I thought maybe the circus was coming and I spent a lot of time at the window looking for the elephants and tigers to show up, but instead of animals a whole bunch of relatives arrived and we had what seemed like a play starring Ellen and Ben in the yard and after that we had a big party in the tent. And if that wasn't enough, the next day we had another big party and I seemed to be the center of attention. I didn't mind all the commotion, especially since I could have all the cake I wanted and everyone laughed when I mashed it all over my face. Grownups really are easy to amuse sometimes. Liam was there too, and we had a chance to play pretty wild in the kitchen one night while the grownups laughed themselves silly again.

Before we left home, the way Mom was packing made me think this trip would be different from the last one. She told Dad we would need at least 19 suitcases to carry everything. Then she proceeded to pack all those wooly things and eskimo clothes she had stashed away in the closet last summer. Of course, at the last minute we had to hurry like crazy to get to the airport by 8 AM, which meant I would miss Sesame Street again; I realized they would cover more of the alphabet while I was gone, and I was afraid I might never find out what comes between "L" and "P". But off we went.

Once I got used to the idea we would be going on an airplane, things seemed to go along pretty smoothly for a while. One thing I like about flying is the fuzzy feeling I get all over; Dad says it's vibration from the engines but whatever it is it sure makes me sleepy. Dad gets sleepy on planes too but I don't think it's vibration that does it for him - it only happens to him after the flight attendant brings him the stuff in the plastic cup. Anyway, I am pretty used to sleeping on planes and once I saw we were flying on USAir again I felt pretty comfortable.

We had to land in Newark to change planes and I remember hanging around the airport there for a while, but that was no big deal because Mom and I had been there lots of times when I was little. The next thing I knew we were up in the air again and pretty soon I heard the pilot say we couldn't land in Albany because of a big snowstorm and we will have to go through to Syracuse. Right away I knew that wasn't the best thing to happen that day because Dad said a few of those words again and Mom told him to hush up.

There was a lot of confusion in the airport at Syracuse and the USAir people didn't seem to know what to do with us. There was talk about taking the Albany passengers there by bus, but nothing happened for a few hours and everybody gave up on that idea. Mom and Dad were both pretty agitated and beforelong they decided to give up on USAir and rent a car to drive to Nan and Pop's house. Then there was a lot of fuss about whether or not it was a good idea to drive in the dark through a blizzard, but finally Dad went to rent a car. Some other guy from our plane asked if he could come along with us and offered to split the costs of the car rental. Mom and Dad said fine but later I wasn't sure what they meant when they said he was lousy at arithmetic. Mom always was one for picking up strays, and she found a young guy at the airport who didn't have any money and she brought him along too which made the car a little crowded but that was OK because it kept it a little warmer.

Finally we were off again and it was pretty late at night by that time. Mom had to drive - I think that was because she was the only one who remembered to bring her driving gloves. it was snowing a lot and I could tell the car was going sideways every now and then, but why should I worry? Sitting in the back in my special seat I was pretty comfortable although I felt like Steve Martin in that silly movie about trying to get home for Thanksgiving. The guy next to me smelled a little bit like I always felt John Candy would smell, especially if he had been traveling all day.

After a real long drive we got to Albany and dropped off our passengers and then drove another long time before we got to Nan and Pop's house. I never did see the river or the woods like it said in my new song. For some reason, Mom stopped singing the song just about the time the pilot said we would have to go to Syracuse.

Pop did have a fire going when we got there, but I don't know what he was burning; the more he burned the colder it got in the house. By the next day so many people had given him a hard time about it that he finally said "OK, OK, turn up the heat!". The big puppy I remembered from the last trip was still there and twice as big but she didn't bite as much anymore. Then who do you think showed up but Liam and we had plenty of time to provide some entertainment again. Which was a good thing because the grown-ups really seemed to need a good laugh.

The End

*As told to his Grandfather 19 years ago by K.G. Younger, now 20 years old.

Shandy's Tales

13

Shandy's Tales

Canaan, New York

Dear Ashley,

Well, I've been in the Berkshires a few months now after spending the first eight years of my life in Maryland. We live way out in the country, which is a lot different from our old place where you used to visit in the suburbs of Washington, D.C. The good part about living there was all the dog cousins that used to come for a visit - like you. Now I don't have any-one to chase around and around Pop's old shed like we used to do. I guess I'm saying I'm not over the homesickness yet.

Otherwise, I like it here - although I must say it does snow quite a bit. There is time to get plenty of rest, which is very important to a dog when he starts getting along in years. But there isn't too much to do compared with back home. There, a lot of people came to the door and I would have to bark for a few minutes at each one; if it was the mailman or the UPS man I was even supposed to put the hair up on my back for a while. I was also responsible for keeping the neighbor's cats out of our yard. Pop hates it when they leave footprints all over his car. But out where we live now people seldom come to the door, and I guess cats can't survive this far north because I haven't seen a single one yet.

After we had been here a month or so I became concerned about having so few responsibilities. I began to worry that maybe my folks will figure I don't earn my keep anymore and start thinking about sending me on my way. I know they like me a lot and I don't think they would do that, but Pop does cuss about the price of dog food every week so you never know. Anyway, I decided to look around for some part-time jobs around the house; nothing strenuous, just enough to look like a working dog.

I thought I should tell you about the job I found. It's no big deal, but Mom and Pop tell everyone about it and last week he even came out before breakfast to shoot about ten pictures of me in action. I'll enclose one of his shots of me trotting up the long driveway with *The Berkshire Eagle* in my mouth. Lucky for me, the guy who delivers the newspaper every morning is real helpful. He puts the paper in a plastic bag and throws it at the end of our driveway. A good thing, too, since the driveway is about 500 dog steps long and I do tend to salivate a lot.

Pop think it's a great job for me and says I take after him; as a kid he had his own route and delivered the *Eagle* every day too, back when it was an afternoon paper. Of course, they take all the credit for teaching this old dog a new trick. Actually, I remember seeing it on a Lassie rerun a few years ago. Anyway, it's not a hard job and I think it's worth the effort; since I started I got a new bed from L.L. Bean and I get an extra treat every morning. And it still leaves plenty of time for rest in front of the big fireplace.

I also want to tell you about the strange thing that happened last week. Maybe you can help me figure it all out. It started Tuesday when I had a big surprise - you'll never guess! Kathy came home for the first time in more than a year; she had never been to our new house before. I heard her tell Gramma that Ken had to go away on a business trip so she decided to visit us. She looked fine - the same as ever really. The funny thing is she brought something with her and I'm still trying to guess what it is.

For now, I'll refer to it as her "little critter" because I figured out pretty quickly that it is alive. At first I thought it was one of those stuffed things she always liked so much, but when no one was looking I poked it with my nose a few times and found out it is soft and warm and smells real funny. Also, it makes a lot of little noises most of the time but sometimes it gets real quiet. Everyone makes a big fuss about this little thing and that makes me even more curious. I can't recall ever seeing anything quite like it before. Well, all that was strange enough, but don't stop reading now. The second big surprise of the week was on Wednesday when - do you believe it? - Ellen came home too. She hadn't been to our new house before either and she also looked real good. She told Gramma that Ben had to stay in New Mexico because he just started a new semester of classes. But - are you ready for this? - Ellen had one of those little critters just like Kathy's.

Like I said, you wouldn't believe the fuss everyone makes over these two little party crashers. Mom can't let either one of them sit still for a minute without scooping it up in her arms and making a lot of silly noises until it laughs at her. Pop calls them "rug rats" but he is real mellow with them too and mostly just lets them lie all over his belly (don't worry, there is plenty of room for both of them). Gramma fusses over them constantly too.

And - believe it or not - on the weekend Mike and Rhonda and Rich and Lisa showed up and they all treated the little nebishes like they were the Royal Family. Watch out, Ashley! Rhonda even talked about getting one of her own but someone said you can't get them in New York.

Yesterday I sat for a long time studying first Kathy's and then Ellen's critter. I'm now convinced they are some new kind of pet that young people consider the "in thing" nowadays.

I still have no idea where they get them, but it does seem like quite a coincidence that both Kathy and Ellen went off to North Carolina and the next thing you know they both come home with one. My guess is they find them in the woods down south. Let me me know what you think.

Write Soon,

Shandy

Whiteout

14

Whiteout

I could make out the tips of my skies as they sliced through the fresh powder, but that was all I could see. I was moving pretty slowly and it didn't make sense to go any faster. Stopping didn't make sense either. So this is what a complete whiteout is all about, I thought. 12,000 feet high in the Rockies, no less. Maybe John Denver would like to write a song about this.

It was my first trip to Arapahoe Basin in Colorado. In fact, it was my first chance ever to ski in the West after a lifetime of battling the boilerplate alternating with slush that passes for snow in the East. Arapahoe sits in the shadow of the 13,204 ft Mt. Lenawee, just west of Loveland Pass, and has long been a favorite of local powderhounds. The upper lifts drop skiers off at just under 12,500 feet, which means most of the earth's atmosphere is below you; it's the highest lift-served skiing in the U.S. The thin air takes some getting used to and it lets almost all the sun's rays through. The snow is something special at these elevations and, as I learned another day, so is the scenery. I learned a few things on this first day, too.

A light snowfall and I arrived in the parking lot at about the same time, and it looked like a great day shaping up. There were only a few other cars in the lot, not so unusual for a Wednesday in April I learned. I took a few warm-up runs on the lower lift and felt fine except for the shortness of breath that the slightest exertion brought on. I found myself stopping every few hundred yards and hanging from my poles as I gasped for the scarce molecules of oxygen; I probably wasn't in the best of shape to begin with, and now my sea level supply of hemoglobin just wasn't getting the job done up here. But I figured I'd take it easy and enjoy the snow, maybe take more breaks than usual for the first few days. So I set off for the top of the mountain.

I literally had the place to myself, and what a place it is. The tree line is just above the beginning of the upper lift, leaving acres and acres of open-slope skiing from the top. Some of the A-Basin terrain is world class - if you doubt my word test your legs on its most famous trail, the Pallavicini, one day! As I settled into my chair there wasn't much visibility, but it didn't seem like anything to get excited about. What should have made an impression on me, but didn't, was that I was the lift's only passenger. Approaching the last lift station the visibility had dropped out the bottom; in an airplane this would definitely be an IFR situation - instruments only. But I guess the cheerful wave from the lift operator in his sturdy little shack at the top was all the reassurance I needed, and without hesitation I was off to attack the Rockies. It slipped my mind that the guy in the shack would be riding down in the chair in any event; no wonder he was cheerful. But here I was and as the saying goes I thought I was in heaven. I didn't know how close I was.

It didn't take me long to realize I was in trouble. After a few hundred yards the snow just seemed to come up and meet me and I was down and sliding. I suddenly realized how little visibility I actually had and how much I depended on visual cues to stay upright. I figured there must be a way around that; after all, I had recently seen a few blind skiers doing just fine. A few hundred yards more and I had that problem sorted out but it suddenly struck me that I had no idea where I was going. The second major lesson for the newcomer to Western skiing: not only is the oxygen scarce above 10,000 feet, but the typical Western area covers more ground than Rhode Island and there are no fences. It would be only too easy to ski out-of-bounds and not be found until spring.

Clearly, I was on the inside of a full-fledged Colorado blizzard. Two more lessons: serious snowstorms can appear without warning in the Rockies and the amount of snow that can fall in an hour will blow the mind of the New Englander who thinks he's seen it all. I couldn't help but notice that this snow was like no snow I had ever skied on before; even with just the tips protruding though the powder, the skis still turned in response to the slightest input. Not like the cream of wheat we called powder in the East. At this point I was still caught up in the euphoria of my first ski trip to the Rockies, but it did cross my mind that I'd like to get back to the lodge and tell the guys about it and so I had better start paying a little more attention to the problem. I had spent a lot of time in the woods of New England, on skis and on foot and even a little on snow shoes, but true whiteouts don't really happen in the east; there is almost always a tree or a bush nearby so at least you always know which way is up. On my first day in the Rockies there were no visual clues whatsoever; the term "lost" took on a new meaning for me. And I had broken a few rules I should have respected; here I was skiing more than two miles high within hours after flying in from sea level, I was skiing alone, and I had left no "flight plan".

By way of formulating a strategy for getting out of this self-created mess, I tried to visualize the layout of the area as it appeared on the trail map. After a few minutes of this, it dawned on me to take the trail map out of my pocket and save the visualizing for tonight's story-telling session around the fireplace. On the southeast side A-Basin is bordered by the Continental Divide; some days later I found that the view from where I stood at that moment was nothing less than sensational. A solid wall of majestic, rocky peaks reaches another 2,000 feet from that spot to divide our continent into two unequal parts. The Lenawee double chair climbs to the top of A-Basin on a path that parallels the mountain wall. On the northwest, the ski area is bordered by a ridge leading down to the tree line; the Norway lift, which I had ridden to the summit is about half-way between the Lenawee chair at the foot of the Continental Divide and the ridge on the west and I figured I had to be between the two lifts.

Luckily I didn't realize it at the time, but my brilliant reasoning had a major flaw; with the visibility as bad as it was, and the chairs as high off the ground as they are, I could easily pass under the lift line and be headed out-of-bounds before I knew it. This is to be avoided even on a clear day; the avalanche threat is even greater when it is snowing like hell. By now there was a good six inches of fresh, glorious, light, crystalline, beautiful, untouched Colorado powder. Unbelievably, at least for a New Englander, 28 inches would fall in less than four hours that day! But at that point I was in no position to enjoy it. My complete attention was devoted to picking my way cautiously downward by letting gravity have its way. I had to assume I was still between the two lift lines and down had to be the way out.

Again, it was better not to be too familiar with the terrain. The next afternoon - a crystal clear "Colorado Day" - I watched a camera crew film a somersaulting skier as he leaped from a small cliff. I must have been quite near that cliff but blithely unaware of its existence. As often happens in life, we end up in the right place for the wrong reason. Visibility didn't improve, but suddenly a lift tower materialized out of the swirling whiteness like Banquo's ghost. At that point I wouldn't be surprised if I kissed the cold green tower, but I don't remember the sensation of my lips sticking to the metal. As I stood there leaning against the beloved man-made tower, I realized that the lifts were silent. No wonder I had felt lost, without visual or aural clues to my location. I was the only one on the mountain, but now I knew how to get down and my thoughts turned to a cold Coors, a hot tub, and a roaring fire. I wasted no time skiing carefully from tower to tower until suddenly the mid-station lodge loomed ahead and the storm started to let up a bit. No one noticed when I walked in. I ordered a beer.

I've skied A-Basin and many other areas in Colorado and Utah since then and the snow continues to amaze me. There is wonderful skiing to be found in the east, my wise cracks not-withstanding - and I head for those hard-packed slopes every chance I get. But the snow is special in the west and the best part is that anyone who grew up skiing in the east will find it a simple matter to adapt to Western conditions. I've taken every opportunity to return to A-Basin, maybe because it is totally unpretentious; if you like the glitz of Aspen then stay on I-70 a little while longer. A-Basin is an area for black dia-mond types who will seek out the steep-n'-deep but, with the wide open spaces letting you pick your own line of descent it is just as great for less ambitious skiers. And the northeastern edge of the area includes the aforementioned world-class Pal-lavicini and some of the best glade skiing I have ever enjoyed.

A-Basin became part of the Keystone complex some years back; the rumors were that the Keystone folks felt they needed to offer more expert terrain to keep up with the com-petition, but the low-key ambiance of earlier days has been retained at the old area. In a way it reminds me a little of ski-ing in the Berkshires in the '50s. Lift tickets don't cost a king's ransom; a stop at the grocery store in Denver would still get you a good discount coupon for A-Basin the last time I was there. And you are buying a ride on snow as light as Utah's best and the elevation means the sunny days are as clear as the aviator's proverbial bell and never too cold unless you are up top where the wind can whip over the ridge.

A-Basin has paid me back since my first visit; every day I have skied there since has been perfect for sun tans and the famous outdoor barbecues halfway up the mountain, yet the snow and the terrain are always the main attractions.

The End

The End

Published by

DayDreamer Press

Viera Florida

www.ingramcontent.com/pod-product-compliance
Lightning Source LLC
Chambersburg PA
CBHW060507030426
42337CB00015B/1773